'LBSC

Footplate Experiences

Reminiscences at New Cross

by
'Curly' Lawrence

Compiled by Klaus Marx

THE OAKWOOD PRESS

British Library Cataloguing in Publication Data
A Record for this book is available from the British Library
ISBN 0 85361 498 9

Typeset by Oakwood Graphics.
Repro by Ford Graphics, Ringwood, Hants.
Printed by D. Brown & Sons Ltd, Bridgend, Mid Glamorgan.

The 3½ in. gauge LB&SCR 'Single' No. 326 *Grosvenor*, probably Lawrence's proudest creation, stands resplendent just off the north curve of his outdoor circuit at Purley Oaks.
Mrs Lorna M. Minton

Title page: 'Curly' Lawrence (*c.* 1882-1967). *Courtesy Brian Hollingsworth*

Published by
The Oakwood Press
P.O. Box 122, Headington, Oxford, OX3 8LU.

Contents

Acknowledgments

It has been a pleasure to edit an illustrated version of Lawrence's serialised 'Recollections of the LB&SC'. Apart from altering a few words here and there to assist the continuity, the script has been left as he wrote it. Chapter headings have been introduced, not an easy task since each instalment contains several diverging anecdotes and experiences.

On the photographic side, it has been possible to illustrate every one of the locomotives mentioned in these memoirs, and for the most part within the compass of the years 1898-1904 when he worked, first as a cleaner and latterly as fireman at New Cross locomotive sheds. These latter again it has been possible to illustrate with hitherto unpublished photographs from the collection of John Minnis. The great majority of illustrations come from two famous LB&SC collections: those of Maurice Bennett, taken personally with his brother Walter in the period between the turn of the century and World War I, and today part of the archives of the Bluebell Railway Preservation Society; and of John L. Smith whose all embracing collection of Brighton locomotive pictures includes the work of distinguished photographers, such as O.J. Morris. The two sharp reproductions of the 3½ in. gauge *Grosvenor* and *Mona* were taken by Mrs Lorna Minton during one of the frequent visits her father paid to the Purley Oaks Light Railway. The LB&SCR Engineman's notice of 1898 was formerly the proud possession of the late Driver George Munn who was fireman aboard *Smeaton* on the record breaking inaugural run of the 'Pullman Limited' that same year, and was presented by his son to the Bluebell Archives. The wonderful photograph on the front cover belonged to Lawrence himself.

Many thanks to all who have enabled me to illustrate every locomotive mentioned individually in Lawrence's script, and also to the late Ralph Stent and to Dick Riley and John Minnis for assistance in identifying and dating most of the pictures and to Peter Winding for help over New Cross Shed and with the accompanying map. I am grateful to Martin Evans, editor of *Model Engineer*, for checking the preface and for kind permission to reprint Lawrence's memoirs. Finally, mention must be made of the help and advice given throughout by the publisher, Jane Kennedy of the Oakwood Press. May this work realise its aim of seeking to do justice to the great individual railwayman that 'Curly' Lawrence was.

Klaus Marx

Preface

Meeting the Author

My acquaintance with 'Curly' Lawrence began in the summer of 1960 at a time when the Bluebell Railway Preservation Society (BRPS) was preparing the wherewithal to commence services at the beginning of August. For some time previously 'Curly' had been following the venture's progress in the national papers and had established contact with David Dallimore, one of the founder members who had charge of the Society's magazine *Bluebell News* during its first five months.

But with the acquisition of the Stroudley 'Terrier' locomotive *Stepney* in May that year, his pleasure knew no bounds, for he wrote

> What a strange coincidence that the BRPS should have acquired the engine I learned to drive when a kid of twelve. In Michael Reynold's book *Locomotive Engine Driving*, he stated that Stroudley engines were so simply constructed and easy to operate, that even a child could drive one. I proved his contention, under the driver's supervision, on the East London line with dear old *Stepney*. Mike was the chief locomotive inspector on the London, Brighton & South Coast Railway (LB&SCR) in those days.

That was in 1894, and it set 'Curly' firmly on the path of the adventures he describes in this book. Even his knowledge of yesteryear was turned to good account. A young Bluebell member wrote in that he had been firing *Stepney* and said she was a shy steamer. 'I put him wise to the fire she liked in East London Line days', 'Curly' remarked. Indeed he was invited to come along to Sheffield Park to drive old *Stepney*, but he never quite got round to this or the other occasions such as the public re-opening. He was elected the first Hon. Member at one of the early meetings and counted it a great honour indeed.

Upon his retirement as an active railwayman he spent most of his later life building small locomotives or writing about them, and his 3½ in. gauge system together with the full-size LB&SCR signal became a familiar landmark on the up side of the Brighton main line just south of Purley Oaks station. Throughout the years he maintained a prodigious output as scores of different designs emerged from his 'Purley Works', and he dealt with an enormous correspondence. In the 'Battle of the Boilers', concerning the power which could be packed into a ½ scale coal-fired locomotive, he demonstrated the ability to build an unbelievable amount of power into a miniature steam locomotive. He was largely responsible in the 1920s for the fillip which boosted live steam clubs up and down the country.

One thing he could never bear was his system being described as a model railway, and for this the uninitiated received a down-to-earth diatribe.

> Now my good friend, just let me correct an erroneous impression on your part. I don't own a 'model railway'. You can buy 'model railways' in toyshops, for children to play with. The Purley Oaks Light Railway is just as much a real railway as the 'Bluebell Line' except for its small size. In fact, it is a few points ahead of the Bluebell in some things,

Dear Marco,
 Afternoons are inconvenient
now,for several reasons (not
naps!)but if you like come
over one evening after 6.45
you can see the railway at
work, and inspect all the
locomotive stock.Perhaps when
the summer holidays are on,
might suit you. When you feel
like it, just ring me for a
date.
 All the best
  Byby

Mr.K.Marx.
67,Bangalore St.
PUTNEY, S.W.15.

The Great Invitation - Curly's postcard of 11th June, 1964.

Inside Lawrence's 'atmospheric' workshop at his house in Purley. In the centre stands his smaller edition of *Grosvenor*. The picture, probably taken by Lawrence, it was presented to the compiler on a visit to his 'railway works'.

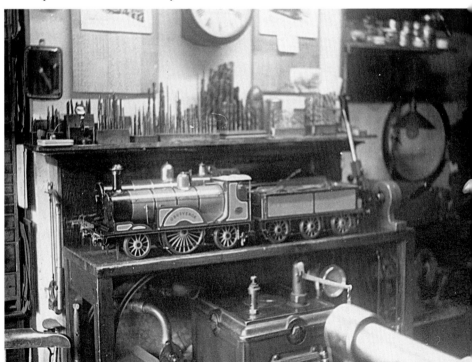

being fully track circuited, with automatic signalling, and possesses a whole fleet of steam locomotives which burn coal and haul loads of living passengers. The types of engines range from a GWR single-wheeler of 1838 to an American Mallet of the 2-6-6-4 articulated type, complete with electric headlight operated by a weeny turbo-generator on the boiler in front of the cab. She can shift three tons. 'Model' - bah!! I hate the sight and sound of the word. I would not describe the outfit under the heading 'Model Railway' for all the tea in China. I should feel that I was insulting it, especially the full-size signal from Coulsdon North.

I did penance by going over to his home early one evening for initiation into his strange world. By this time he was past his 80th birthday. He greeted me in his chirpy personal manner, wearing a little black beret, and hobbled down the corridor to show me 'the Works'. The little back room was a miracle of compactness, no machine shop could have been laid out with more precision in the space available. In addition to the rows of tools on their trays and shelves, he had managed to fit in a large number of railway relics - LBSC of course! 'That ring on the wall on the right is one of *Denmark*'s ('Terrier' No. 39) cab window frames. The clock over the shelf came from the old wooden station at Streatham Common.' He then ushered me to the cupboard under the stairs and asked me to peer inside. It was packed with miniature locomotives, well into double figures. We lingered over a 'super Arthur' - numbered Southern Railway 870 I believe - and then went out of doors for the special treat he had in store for, knowing my 'Brighton' leanings, he had *Grosvenor* already lit up, quietly simmering by the large 'Brighton' lower quadrant signal. I believe No. 326 was his special pride too, judging by the loving way he spoke about it.

She upholds the Stroudley traditions - I'll say she does! She treats my weight, equal to 17 coaches, like a bag of birds feathers and has run nearly two miles on a single firing, with the lever notch to middle, speed equalling about 75 mph. She is 3½ in. gauge (one-sixteenth of full size) and was built about 17 years ago. I did not need any drawings, knowing practically every nut and bolt in the Brighton engines. Externally she is an exact replica of her big sister, but the 'works' are in accordance with modern practice, as she has long-travel valves, uses superheated steam, mechanical lubrication and an injector - you can see it behind the trailing wheel - to supplement the usual crosshead pump. She thinks nothing of making a non-stop run of four miles or more, hauling my weight (equal to a 320 ton train), burning a mixture of hard and Welsh coal, and the safety-valves on the sizzle all the time with 80 lb. on the clock. The blast when running is almost inaudible.

After testing *Grosvenor* over a few circuits, he was ready to invite me to take my seat on the flat wagon hauled in its wake, and away we sailed, gently accelerating, occasionally sparing a wave at the puzzled human faces pressed against the window panes of the passing electric trains. 'Ten laps on a mere shovelful of coal', he gleamed as we came to rest by the signal in the gathering darkness.

It was only after we had completed our trip that he tactfully divulged that his little railway was not in the best of shape. It was also having its share of PW and maintenance problems.

A study of 'Terrier' No. 39 *Denmark* (named after the Denmark Hill area in South London) standing in immaculate condition at Battersea Shed at the turn of the century. One of the latter's cab window frames was a permanent fixture inside Lawrence's 'Purley Works'. *Lens of Sutton*

By comparison with Lawrences's 3½ in. gauge LBSC 'Single', the real *Grosvenor* awaiting departure at Hove with a return working to Victoria in 1903.   *O.J. Morris Collection*

After nearly 30 years of the British climate, wood girders are springy and rotting, and in three places it is giving under the load. They are cutting up a lot of old wooden wagons at Ashford Works, and as some of the timber is still sound and well seasoned, the sawmill foreman is cutting some new girders for me, so I can replace my defective ones. The compressor for supplying air to operate the old LB&SCR signal conked out last week with a busted valve, so there was another little job waiting. Misfortunes never come singly.

Back inside the cosy workroom we moved on from Stroudley to Billinton. A year or so previously, the BRPS had acquired *Birch Grove* which again pleased him no end. 'I knew her well when she was at New Cross at the turn of the century. I forget for the minute who drove her, but the cleaner's name was Gear. Some of the boys called him 'Cogwheel'.
He went on:

I just love taking a design which was either inefficient or a complete failure, cutting out the faults, and making a real good engine. Having worked on the Billinton radial tanks, I knew their faults all right (I'll say I did). The other picture shows what they would have looked like if I'd had old Bob's job. A bigger boiler with superheater (say about 200 lb. pressure), 20 in. cylinders, mechanical lubrication, and a much better arrangement of valves and valve setting. They wouldn't half have made the suburban trains step lively.
The little one is 3½ in. gauge and can get away with half-a-dozen adult passengers like an electric. The sharp cracks of the exhaust would bring joy to the heart of any driver. She can run so fast that you can hardly see the coupling-rods, some difference to old Bob's contraptions.

Over the boiler store on the 'erecting bench' stood his latest effort, GWR 'Dukedog' No. 9015. 'Her name is *Dilys*. I called her that as the class finished their days in Wales, and *Dilys* was the shortest Welsh girls' name I could think of, and the easiest to put on a nameplate.' I told him it was a pity about the number, but he had already started on the project before No. 9017 arrived at the Bluebell Railway.
His latest project, still on the drawing board, was a design for a 3½ in. gauge edition of the class '9' 2-10-0 locomotive *Evening Star*, the last locomotive to be built for British Railways. He was not able to attend the naming ceremony at the personal invitation of the Western Region Area Board, but Swindon sent him a pile of drawings of the full-size engine. But it was not as simple as it sounded.

A reduced copy of the full-size job would be useless as a working proposition, as Nature won't be scaled, and scheming out the little *Evening Star*, capable of pulling at least a dozen adults continuously, was some job. I'm up to my neck getting out the valve gear. It took the whole drawing office staff at Brighton to get out the valve gear for the full size 2-10-0 engine, so you can imagine what I'm up against with this little one. It is impossible to scale down, as the dimensions would then be unworkable, e.g. the full-size eccentric rods are 5 ft 3²⁵⁄₆₄ in. long, and you can work out for yourself what ⅟₁₆th of that would be. For a guaranteed-to-work job I have to re-design the whole of the gear, yet have to keep it looking the same as big sister. I guarantee all my instructions, and it is a fact, and not hot air, to say that more locomotives have been built to my designs (all successful) than those of any full-size CME from Trevithick to the present day.

To hear anyone speak in such terms might deserve a stricture for gross conceit, but there was never a trace of this in 'Curly' Lawrence, for he was shy and modest, almost a recluse in his later years, and declining the many occasions when people sought to do him honour. What was truly remarkable and is borne out in the pages that follow, was the high standard of literary talent from one who entered the railway service as a lad without completing his education. He was a self-taught man with a ready gift for a turn of phrase, and this soon became apparent in his articles in the *Model Engineer* which he wrote almost continuously from September 1924 until his death. These brought him fame and friends, but did not receive widest recognition until the post-war years. Offers piled in from publishers, even the 'Cheesecake Press' as he put it, bid for his life story, but he turned down the lot. The nearest he came to this was his contribution in *Simple Model Locomotive Building*, introducing LBSC's *Tich*, published in 1968, shortly after his death, with a foreword by Martin Evans, the Editor of the *Model Engineer*. This present book seeks to reduce the imbalance and give Lawrence the credit that was really his due.

Right to the end 'Curly' Lawrence preferred the anonymity of his pen-name 'LBSC' and under the title 'Recollections of the LB&SCR' he contributed regular instalments in *Bluebell News* between 1960 and 1962. They are written in a classic vein as far as railway literature goes, and to find an engineman writing with such clarity and interest is rare gold indeed. The language and mannerism of the engine driver are draped in the most exact English - few indeed were the mistakes or dots out of place in his copy or his letters - and he had the attribute of rendering his slang quite respectable. He spoke of his contributions as 'dope' or another 'spasm'; he lived in the world of his youth - a car for him was always a 'gas-buggy' - and the railway lingo was part and parcel of his thinking. For example, on being asked to make some prediction about the following year, he replied 'It would take a darn good driver to see twelve sections ahead'.

One recalls a splendid return of serve which the Reverend Awdry received, after writing: 'I am particularly delighted with LBSC's recollections. I hope that neither he nor you will mind, but I have snaffled one, which suitably adapted, will appear in my next 'Thomas' book (The local Whillie paid a call at the Station-Master's house!)' The generous but off-hand reply came back from 'Curly': 'It is quite OK by me for his Reverence to sneak my recollection of old *Cliftonville*'s uninvited call on the station master for use in his book. In fact, he can make what use he likes of any of them, as far as I'm concerned. Glad he finds them interesting'.

But others were not so lucky, and he had occasional brushes with the publishing press, and particularly over printer's errors. His complaint over their concoction of a 'distance' signal, incidentally, led to succinct explanations of which the following on LBSC signalling is a fine example of his art.

The three basic signals in a block section on the LB&SCR were 'distant', 'home' and 'starting'. There were also auxiliary signals, such as outer and inner home, advance starter, calling-on, shunt and crossover signals, the latter being known as 'dummies' or 'tommy-dods'. There were also platform repeaters, which were miniature working signals located close to the base of the full-size signals, for the benefit of the fogman who didn't have to look aloft through fog. Distant signals were distinguished from stop signals by having a notch in the end of the arm, and before the advent of the yellow lights, many also had the Welsh - Coligny patent lamps which showed a white chevron alongside the usual green or red aspect. LB&SCR signalmen never pulled off the distant signal until the whole section was clear and the stop signals off.

It could hardly have been summarised more clearly within so small a compass - and by a man in his early-eighties.

In his last years he reluctantly but realistically curtailed his literary sorties. 'At my time of life I'm not particularly keen on doing more writing.' Offers to write books poured in as his talents received belated recognition. He turned them down. But one small tribute he greatly appreciated was the gesture made by the engine crews of 'The Scottish Belle' special which brought the famous Caledonian Single No. 123 down for a once-and-for-all visit to the South of England on 15th September, 1963. 'I saw the old "Caley" and the "Greyhound" go by on the Sunday trip down to the Bluebell', Curly wrote. 'On the return journey both engines blew their whistles like hell and the arabs on the footplate waved as they went by here. I guess somebody put them up to it!'

Though he may have curtailed his writing, he remained active to the last at his work bench. In one of his last letters he wrote:

I'm still at it. Finished a 3½ in. 'Dukedog' last spring, since then have built a LMS 0-6-0 (class '4') and am now well away with a L&NWR Jumbo (2-4-0) and a Southern 'S15' (4-6-0). I can build two together as easily as one, and nearly as quickly. When finished, there will be 23 in my running shed. Probably I shall still be building them when I get a telegram from the Queen. No diesels on our road, and Dr Beeching can't shut it down.

And he never forgot about old *Stepney*. In almost his last letter he requested: 'Next time you see old *Stepney*, give her my love and tell her it's from the kid with the long golden curls who learned to drive her on the East London line, way back in 1894. Boy-oh boy, does time roll on!'

He died shortly afterwards, near the end of 1967, somewhat short of receiving his anticipated 'telegram from the Queen'.

'E4' class No. 473 *Birch Grove* (named after a hamlet and mansion near Horsted Keynes and today preserved at the nearby Bluebell Railway) is prepared for duty outside the Middle Shed at New Cross early in the present century. Behind No. 473 in the shed doorway stands 'E3' class No. 456 *Aldingbourne*. *M.P. Bennett/Bluebell Archives*

Lawrence's idea of a 'super' Billinton radial tank engine, standing outside his locomotive shed (*to left*). *Mona* was a simple 3½ in. gauge 0-6-2T with Hackworth valve gear. In the background is the embankment of the Brighton main line. *Mrs Lorna M. Minton*

'Curly' Lawrence

Some Biographical Notes

Brian Hollingsworth in his book *'LBSC' His Life and his Locomotives*, which is largely given to close coverage of Lawrence's creations and innovations in the field of locomotive model engineering, like all of us found 'Curly' (so called for his fine youthful head of long golden curls) 'an enigmatic and private person.' Brian has carefully investigated the story of his birth and early days and come to the conclusion that Lawrence was born around 1882 and spent his early childhood in Peckham. He received an excellent education in the independent sector which laid the basis of his later flair for fluent writing and his brilliant grasp of mathematics and engineering. He displayed an early and precocious interest in transport, building his first steam locomotive whilst still a youngster at school.

An opportune moment, as he relates at the beginning of these reminiscences, won him the friendship of his local station master at Queen's Road, Peckham, and contact with a friendly driver from New Cross depot led to his inaugural footplate trip on 'Terrier' No. 55 *Stepney* up the East London line to Shoreditch. He was 'sold' on steam locomotives and in the mid-1890s joined the London Brighton & South Coast Railway to start his apprenticeship at New Cross as a cleaner boy at two shillings (10p) per day. How far he got up the ladder 'Curly' never let out, though his autobiographical material gives the impression of firing and driving locomotives. Certainly he started in a cleaner gang of half a dozen lads working under a supervisor from 6 am to 5.30 pm with a 45 minute break for breakfast and 60 minutes for lunch. In the seven or so years of railway service he would only have graduated to approved fireman, but that status would have enabled him to go out on the road. His amazing instant grasp of the intimate working of the steam locomotive in its railway setting was noted early when, after the 1899 Bermondsey collision in fog, he offered proposals for a cab signalling system which the powers that be did not follow up.

In 1902 he began to write articles for the *Model Engineer* under the pseudonym 'J M W Peckham' where 'Curly' lived. By now he was finding more satisfaction in his model engineering, and the grimy taxing locomotive work held less attraction for him. He moved on to the London Underground as a driver of its recently introduced electric trains. This was short-lived when on health grounds his doctor advised him to take a job in the open air. So around 1904 he turned to driving trams from Rye Lane depot, and a further few years on forsook the rails to drive motor buses.

Married in January 1908, Mr and Mrs Lawrence moved into a flat in Dulwich. In 1910 he took a job with the Daimler Motor Car Co., commuting by train the 90 miles to Coventry daily. His next job was a travelling inspector for Messrs Thomas Tilling, the London based transport firm. He and Mabel were now able to afford a rented house close to Norbury station. 'Curly' was exempted on occupational grounds from military service in the Great War, but did his bit by managing a small munitions factory at Weybridge producing aero-engine parts. He returned to his pre-war job, adding a supplementary income by repairing mechanical items and building locomotives for client friends.

His real break in the world of model engineering came in 1922 in 'The Battle of the Boilers', and led him into his *chef d'oeuvre* of instruction on the building of small locomotives. He was soon inundated with requests for information from people interested in that hobby. The Norbury Light Railway which he had set up in his garden was shortlived as a developer bought the properties near the station for turning into shops and offices. This turned 'Curly's' mind towards the other side of the Atlantic. He sailed to the United States in January 1930 and was found a residence in Greenwich, Connecticut by an admiring professional engineer. His host gave 'Curly' the freedom of his own miniature railway, but by July he and Mabel were back in this country for good.

The decade that followed proved the vintage years of 'Curly's' output. He had moved to a new home alongside the Brighton main line just south of Purley Oaks station and negotiated for a plot adjacent to the railway fence that was too narrow for building further houses on the east side of Grange Road. On it he constructed and operated the Purley Oaks Light Railway which must have intrigued many a passenger in passing trains from which a grandstand view could be obtained.

World War II brought little interruption to his business and writings, though he endured the blitz and ensuing raids with all his fellow Londoners.

The arrival of the 'V1' flying bombs in 1944 led the Lawrences to evacuate temporarily to Stourbridge and on to friends at Stafford, but by September they had returned home.

'Curly' continued his locomotive construction and written contributions, finding age no handicap. But in 1959 he fell out with the new generation of senior staff of the *Model Engineer* and switched to the *Model Maker*. 'Curly' intimated he had stayed his pen over the question of a rise in the rate of remuneration. He said the managing director refused to budge, stating there were plenty of others who could write in the same vein. Lawrence went on strike and sales of the *Model Engineer* dropped so appreciably that it was not too long before he began to write for Martin Evans, its new editor, at three times his former remuneration. Such was his pull amongst the model engineering fraternity. This whole affair elicited a host of support and letters from admirers from all parts of the world but never really sweetened the pill of that self-enforced retirement. From that time he tended to close in on himself, continuing to build locomotives within the confines of his workshop. Sustained by the royalties from his books and plans, he now invited only the closest of his circle of friends over to 121, Grange Road where lengthy discussions on the ins-and-outs of model engineering were held in his spick and span workshop, or a visitor's favourite locomotive selected for a run outside.

But he was feeling his age and became tired more quickly than heretofore. His first really serious illness in his life came early in 1967 with a bout of pneumonia and a brief stay in Croydon's Mayday Hospital. Despite seeming recovery, several relapses followed and he died peacefully in his sleep on 5th November, 1967, arriving as he once put it, at 'the terminal station of the Great Railroad of Life.' Mabel carried on at No. 121 until 1969 and, following spells in a Nursing Home, died in 1972.

Shall we ever see his like again? Lawrence had the genius quality of inspiring people, and his reminiscences are a distinctive and attractive trademark in an era when next to no railwaymen were putting pen to paper.

I am indebted to Brian Hollingsworth for allowing me to summarise from his book the salient facts of 'Curly's' life story.

New Cross Depot

New Cross was the 'Brighton's' premier locomotive depot in London for the company's emphasis, prior to the construction into Victoria in 1860 followed by the Battersea Park Shed complex a decade later, was from the outset totally based on serving London Bridge. The London & Croydon Railway had purchased from the virtually defunct Croydon & Rotherhithe Canal Company several acres of land which provided the site of a railway complex with plenty of scope for future expansion. The first locomotives were being delivered in the summer of 1838 and services between Croydon and London Bridge commenced on 5th June, 1839, the London & Croydon's first buildings for a locomotive shed and workshops being opened four days previously.

The immediate period that followed was one of uncertainty in direction as first in 1842 the South Eastern and the London & Croydon decided to pool their rolling stock under a management known as the Joint Locomotive Committee, being joined two years later by the Brighton company, then seriously short of serviceable engines and repair facilities. The Joint Committee designated New Cross as its principal workshops under the direction of Benjamin Cubbitt. The pooling arrangement led to bickering and disagreements, and from 31st January, 1846 the three constituents chose to go their separate ways again with an appropriate redistribution of stock. The South Eastern was in the process of constructing its own shops at nearby Bricklayers Arms and was soon to begin at Ashford, while the Brighton company was developing its works' site adjacent to the southern terminus of its line. The depot at New Cross had at this time suffered a temporary setback on the night of 14th October, 1844 when a large fire broke out completely destroying the original roundhouse (one of the earliest in the country), known as the 'Octagon' together with a number of engines. The turntable and radiating roads survived to be incorporated into a repair shop.

The other element of uncertainty at this time lay with Mr Samuda's atmospheric experiment on the Croydon Railway, a brave initiative which it was realised all too soon suffered under too many handicaps compared with steam traction. The line consisted of an extra track laid from Croydon to New Cross where the terminal facilities were located. Peter Winding suggests that the old 'Croydon' Shed which lay next to the up local line may have been built as a train shed to serve as a through station when services should be extended to London Bridge. But before this could happen the atmospheric venture was cut short and remained a bone of contention after the Croydon and Brighton companies merged on 27th July, 1846 to form the London Brighton and South Coast Railway. The former Croydon Directors on the new Board fought a bitter rearguard action on the issue. The above mentioned shed which had been built by the London & Croydon Company was soon after converted to house steam locomotives and continued to be known thereafter as the 'Croydon' Shed, though also on occasions as the 'Long' Shed.

By 1850 the new company had constructed opposite the northern end of the Croydon Shed another straight and single-ended shed comprising three roads, the original 'Middle' Shed which was destroyed by a great storm in 1863. It was quickly reconstructed to the same dimensions and layout a few months later with a long two-road carriage shed to its rear. Most of this cast-iron

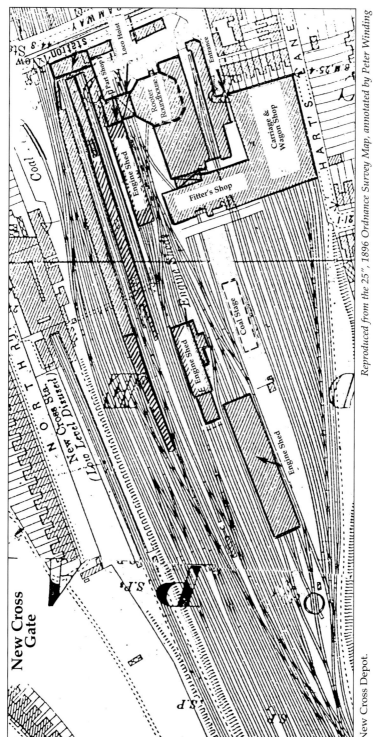

New Cross Depot.

Reproduced from the 25″, 1896 Ordnance Survey Map, annotated by Peter Winding

construction was removed in the 1880s, but a section that abutted the back of the engine shed was retained as a fitters' shop until 1949. By 1860 two separate 40 ft turntables were in use.

In the early 1870s William Stroudley added his famous 'Rooter Roundhouse' which served to accommodate his diminutive 'Terriers' in today's parlance, but known as 'Rooters' to the enginemen of those days, a baker's dozen of which were used on the busy South and East London lines respectively. It was octagonal in plan with two roads to each bay with a turntable so small that the tracks off the pit actually overlapped each other providing an extremely cramped layout. By World War I nearly all the 12 ft wheelbase 'Terriers' had left for the country and, as no other class could be accommodated, it fell out of use as an engine shed, serving as an adjunct to the workshops as a boiler shop or store siding.

With the considerable expansion of the LB&SCR in the 1870s and especially in south London with an accompanying increase in new train services, the erstwhile facilities at New Cross were proving inadequate and a programme of additional building for the repair and maintenance of locomotives and rolling stock was becoming imperative. After some hesitation and delay the Brighton Board authorised the necessary expenditure for new works carried out between 1881 and 1883, the main feature being a new four-road engine shed adjacent but immediately north of the Middle Shed. Completed in 1882, this had through roads which led at the north end onto a new 50 ft turntable. Known as the 'New'

A photograph taken by Dr A.C. Hovenden, one of a series taken at New Cross Shed on 14th September, 1901, shows the Croydon Shed exterior to advantage with its whitened wall and round-arched paned windows giving it more of the appearance of a chapel. It forms a backcloth to the New Cross breakdown crane No. 316S built in 1898 by Cowans, Sheldon, which stands in the old works yard. Behind is the rest of the breakdown train comprising two very old converted Craven carriages between which is an open goods 'A' wagon bearing a tarpaulin marked 'Loco Dept, New Cross'.   *John Minnis Collection*

Shed, it was, like its companions, of brick construction with pitched slate roofs. Carriage and wagon repair shops were erected behind the terrace of houses in Brighton Grove, built in earlier days to provide housing for railway employees, but long since insufficient, the great majority of New Cross men living some way from the depot and often in lodgings. Another improvement at this time was the installation of an engine hoist over the two roads that lay between the Rooter Roundhouse and the paint shop at the rear of the Croydon Shed.

Looking back, despite its importance the whole complex had developed in a very piecemeal fashion into an awkwardly laid out depot which must not have been the easiest to operate in its crowded heyday, particularly as it involved the despatch and return of locomotives across the set of heavily used running lines to the eastern side occupied by both goods and carriage sidings. 'Curly' Lawrence was undoubtedly in the vicinity of one such accident to which he devotes one of his episodes. This occurred on 13th June, 1899 involving light engine No. 139 *Lombardy* moving across the main running lines and colliding with a passenger train hauled by 'D' tank No. 224 *Crowhurst*.

Thankfully these were the last major alterations of any consequence and provided the New Cross Shed scene with which 'Curly' Lawrence would have

The scene captured by Dr Hovenden at twenty minutes past midday on 14th September, 1901. The clock stands at a central viewpoint for all three sheds, affixed by some fine ironwork tracery brackets to the upper storey of the office of the shed foreman. The latter is probably the bowler hatted figure talking to a member of staff, while an engineman wistfully watches colleagues going off duty and passing the east side of the fitters' shop. Two 'Gladstones' and a radial tank stand alongside and in front of the Middle Shed whilst a domeless SER 4-4-0 pulls out of New Cross station in the direction of London Bridge.

John Minnis Collection

Dr Hovenden moves round the corner to gain a closer view of the array of locomotives standing outside the New and Middle Sheds. These include Billinton 'B2' 4-4-0s, 'D' class 0-4-2Ts and a radial tank. The 'gaffer's' attention is directed to something to his left where the coal siding and stack are located.   *John Minnis Collection*

Dr Hovenden next moved on towards the turntable which was sited at the north end of the New Shed where 'D3' class 0-4-4T No. 389 *Shoreham* of Tunbridge Wells Shed is about to be turned for its return journey to Kent. The East London line is on the left and the East London Up Junction signal box of 1876 is seen behind the solitary coach.   *John Minnis Collection*

An even closer view of the New and Middle Sheds shows 'D3' class No. 396 *Clayton* as yet unrebuilt, standing by the coaling stage. Coaling was by crane from the wagons on the extreme left. Other identifiable locomotives include a relatively new class 'E5' which appears to be No. 568 *Carisbrooke* (one of several in the class converted temporarily by Marsh to 2-4-2T), and in the adjacent road 'E1' class 0-6-0T No. 151 *Helvetia* and 'D3' class No. 373 *Billingshurst*, all New Cross-based engines; in the far road is 'B2' class 4-4-0 No. 322 *G.P. Bidder* of Portsmouth shed on a visit up to London. Through the slight smoke haze can be discerned the forge and lean-to at the side of the Middle Shed.

The late H.M. Madgwick Collection

A sunny midday scene, possibly on a Sunday, when things were relatively quiet and outside the Middle Shed stand line upon line of locomotives. On the left stands 'E5' class 0-6-2T No. 587 (formerly *Brighton*) which was based at the shed of that name but is strictly 'Not To Be Moved'. Marsh 'C3' class 0-6-0 No. 304 joined the New Cross allocation on 3rd July, 1906, class 'D3X' No. 396, looking good as new, was rebuilt by Marsh using an 'I2' pattern boiler in April 1909, while on the far right road is 'E3' class 0-6-2T No. 456 (formerly *Aldingbourne*), also a New Cross engine. Two cleaner boys in the centre of the picture look the photographer's way.

The late H.M. Madgwick Collection

The scene inside the old Croydon Shed prior to demolition taken in June 1947. The photographer stands within the confines of the old paint shop which comprised its rear section. Straight ahead lies the Middle Shed and, beyond it to its right, New Cross Yard signal box.

Peter Winding

The 'Rooter Roundhouse' seen here, was built for 'Terriers' in the early 1870s and is not to be confused with the original octagonal roundhouse which was part of the London & Croydon Railway Works. On 4th March, 1939 'D1' class 0-4-2T No. 2357 (old *Riddlesdown*) has found a quiet corner for a lay by, but members of the class would never have used the roundhouse as the small central turntable could only accommodate a 'Terrier' with its smaller wheelbase. Even prior to the war the roof was in a thoroughly decrepit and slateless state. *H.C. Casserley*

This 1948 photograph shows the old 'Rooter Roundhouse' from a slightly different angle. On the right is the old erecting shop and former timber store, on the left the side of the old Croydon Shed and in the centre locomotives stand under the engine hoist where *Cliftonville*, as related on page 33, ended up in the station master's house beyond. *Peter Winding*

A nostalgic portrait taken from the interior of the wagon workshop sited opposite to the Croydon Shed. A crank axle and shaft of a driving wheel languish in 1947 on the entrance road leading to the wagon turntable.   *Peter Winding*

been all too familiar. The allocation of 114 locomotives, almost exactly a quarter of the Brighton company's capital stock of 458, for 1896, soon after he joined, are listed in the accompanying table. New Cross was to reach a peak of 167 locomotives on its books by 1911, making it the largest of the company's depots.

At the 1923 Grouping the name was changed to New Cross Gate to avoid confusion with the ex-SER station barely 500 yards away to the east. Soon came the inevitable decline, accelerated by progressive electrification, and by the end of World War II the depot was looking very tumbledown and sorry for itself after sustaining extensive wartime damage. Much of the missing roofing was never replaced and stored locomotives stood in the shells of once proud buildings. The first stage of closure commenced at the end of 1946 with the transfer away of much of its allocation. The depot officially closed in June 1947 though some locomotives still continued to be serviced there and repairs still took place in the workshops into nationalisation days. All this eventually ceased on 23rd May, 1949 leaving a collection of stored locomotives and a concentration of wagon repairs in the adjacent workshops. Demolition of most of the locomotive servicing area and buildings took place in 1957. Only a few of the original workshop buildings Lawrence knew still survive in engineering use, but for the most part the area now comprises sidings for the servicing and storage of emu stock. In one sense the railway lives on, but gone forever is that thriving turn-of-the-century community of which an observant 'Curly' Lawrence was part.

New Cross Locomotive Allocation 1896

Stroudley Classes		Nos.	Total	Duties
'A1'	0-6-0T	49/50/2-62	13	Inner suburban passenger
'B1'	0-4-2	173/7/90/1/4/5/217	7	Express passenger
'C'	0-6-0	409/10/1/9	4	Goods workings
'C1'	0-6-0	425/31	2	Goods workings
'D1'	0-4-2T	7-11/20/227/40-4/59-64 279/85/7/8/98/9/355-361	31	Suburban and stopping passenger
'D2'	0-4-2	302/3/9/11/3	5	Mixed traffic
'E1'	0-6-0T	85-8/94-6/103/11/5/7 122/5/31/2/7-9/40/1/5/7 149/151/3/4/6/62/3	29	Shunting and short goods trips
'G'	2-2-2	328/30/1/3/46-8	7	Express passenger

R. Billinton Classes				
'C2	0-6-0	433/4/45/6/50/1	6	Goods workings
'D3'	0-4-4T	368/70/3/5/82/8/96	7	Outer suburban passenger
'E3	0-6-2T	453/6/60	3	Goods workings

Total   114

LONDON BRIGHTON AND SOUTH COAST RAILWAY COMPANY.

LOCOMOTIVE DEPARTMENT.

TERMS OF SERVICE FOR ENGINEMEN AND FIREMEN.

1.—TIME.

In future, Drivers and Firemen will be paid at the rate of 10 hours per day, or sixty hours for six days; time to be taken when they come on duty by order, and when they leave duty according to the instructions of each Foreman respectively.

No man will be paid less than six days for one week's work (exclusive of Sunday) unless off duty on his own account.

No man shall receive less than one day's pay after being booked on duty, except for Shed work as provided for in paragraph 4, or when booked on twice in one day; in which latter case he will be paid a minimum of 1½ day's wages for the two turns of duty.

2.—OVERTIME.

Overtime to be reckoned as the excess of sixty hours per week of six days, and paid at the rate of eight hours per day.

3.—SUNDAY DUTY.

Sunday duty to be calculated at the rate of eight hours per day, and allowed to those men who book on duty between Saturday midnight and Sunday midnight, for the hours worked during that period.

No man shall receive less than one day's pay for Sunday duty.

4.—SHED DUTY.

Men who run 750 miles or upwards in five days, shall have a Shed day once a week, or as near to that as can be arranged. This Shed day to be reckoned as ten hours' work.

Other Drivers and Firemen when required for Shed duty, such as washing out their Boilers, &c., will be allowed five hours' pay.

5.—TIME OFF DUTY.

So far as the necessities of the Service will permit, nine hours, at least, off duty to be arranged for.

6.—WAGES.

In future, all Drivers and Firemen joining the Service will be paid the following scale of Wages:—

	Drivers.	Firemen.
1st Year, per day	5s. 6d.	3s. 6d.
2nd ,, ,,	6s.	3s. 9d.
3rd ,, ,,	6s. 6d.	4s.
4th ,, ,,	6s. 6d.	4s.
5th ,, ,,	7s.	4s. 3d.
6th ,, ,,	7s.	
7th ,, ,, For Main Line Passenger and Goods men, if employed regularly as such for twelve months previously.	7s. 6d.	

A fair proportion of long-service Drivers and Firemen may be advanced, if their characters are satisfactory, to 7s. 6d. and 8s.; and 4s. 6d. and 4s. 9d. per day respectively.

The highest ordinary rate for Shunters to be 6s. per day; but a portion of them having the most responsible duties may be advanced to 7s. per day.

When a Fireman has been passed as Driver, he will receive 4s. 6d. per day; and when a Cleaner has been passed as Fireman, he will be paid 3s. per day.

All advances to be subject to the District Locomotive Superintendent's report as to good conduct and ability; and may be deferred at the discretion of the Locomotive Superintendent; in which case the men shall be advised by letter, giving the reason why such advance is deferred.

7.—LODGING ALLOWANCE.

Drivers and Firemen when absent from home will be allowed 2s. 6d. per night, the maximum allowance for one week being 6s.

8.—PROMOTION.

Promotion to be by seniority and merit. Economical working and proper care of the engine, together with punctuality in time, to have due weight.

9.—SUSPENSION FROM DUTY.

The Company reserves the right of suspending from duty any Driver or Fireman in case of accident or misconduct, pending the decision of the case by the Directors, Government Inspectors, or other authority. District Locomotive Superintendents have the power to suspend from duty; but dismissal or reduction to be by order of the Locomotive Superintendent. Breaches of discipline, misconduct, mismanagement of engine or train, damage or injury caused, may be punished by dismissal or by reduction.

10.—CLOTHING.

An Overcoat to be given every alternate year to each Driver and Fireman, and a Cap every year; the last Coat and Cap given to be returned to the Company in the event of a man leaving the Service.

11.—LEAVING THE SERVICE.

Seven days' notice must be given on either side, except in cases of misconduct, when the Company reserves the right of instant dismissal.

12.—PREMIUMS AND BENEFITS.

Coal and Oil Premiums are allowed to Drivers as per printed scale.

Drivers must join the Superannuation Fund, and Drivers and Firemen should also become Members of the Provident Society and Insurance Fund in connection with this Company.

BRIGHTON WORKS,
1st January, 1898.

R. J. BILLINTON,
Locomotive Superintendent.

LB&SCR notice of 1898 showing terms of service for enginemen and firemen.
Courtesy George Munn

Chapter One

Learning the LBSC 'Family' Trade

It was in 1890 that I first made the acquaintance of a Brighton engine's footplate. As a child, I used to run a four-wheeled toy locomotive with a spirit-fired boiler and oscillating cylinders on the footpath of the street in South London where I lived. This attracted the attention of the local station master, who resided close by. I always took a short cut through the station on my way to and from school, and one afternoon I saw him talking to a driver. It was windy and some papers he was holding blew out of his hand. I retrieved them, and he introduced me to the driver and told him about my toy engine.

The driver was interested, and that evening took me for a trip on the East London line on 'Terrier' No. 55 *Stepney*. It was the first of several. He taught me all about her, and when I left school he sponsored my application for a cleaner's job at the local sheds. I had already made the acquaintance of other enginemen and some of the staff, so I started work among friends.

In those far-off days the LB&SCR was a sort of happy family. Relations between officials and workers was of the best. Everything was 'free-and-easy'. The depots were known just as running-sheds, or steam sheds, not 'motive power depots'. The boss was known as 'the bloke' and his understudy 'the gaffer'. They knew all the enginemen's nicknames, and used them. If the boss or the foreman ever called a driver or fireman by anything other than his first name or nickname, it was reckoned a sure sign that he was going to be 'carpeted' for something or other! Work was hard and the hours long, but nobody seemed to mind. In fact, some of the enginemen were not satisfied unless they could squeeze a fortnight's work on to a week's pay ticket. Night goods crews booking off in the early morning would go home and get a little sleep, then come back and work excursions, race specials and so on, at overtime rate. As their time was their own between arrival on the outward trip, and departure on the return trip, they were easily able to get sufficient rest. It seemed to work all right, as nobody ever had a pitch-in through falling asleep in the cab! Anyway, there were always plenty of volunteers for the specials.

Cleaners started at 2s. 2d. per day, and rose to 3s. When passed for firemen, they received 3s. 6d. per day, rising to 5s. 6d. Firemen received 6s. on being passed as drivers. The top rate for main line drivers was 8s. per day. This does not sound much as things are at the present time; but it really purchased more than present day wages. When 'fags' were five for a penny, twopence bought a pint of 'wallop', a few shillings went a very long way.

I knew of a driver's wife - a plump jolly Lancashire woman - who used to provide board and lodging for cleaners. She never had any children of her own, and as her house was large enough to accommodate them, she was never happy unless she had five or six 'adopted sons' to look after. She fed them well, did all their washing (including overalls) and mending, all for - hold your breath! - five shillings and sixpence per week. It is hardly necessary to add that the boys loved their 'mum' and frequently bought her presents.

Cleaner gang at New Cross in 1898, a photograph Lawrence treasured all his days. 'Terrier' No. 52 *Surrey* was the shed pilot at the time and, according to D.L. Bradley, seldom ventured further afield because of its poor mechanical order. *Surrey*'s Stroudley gamboge livery contrasts with the lined green of the 'C2' class 0-6-0 next in line.   *L. Lawrence Collection*

'Terrier' 0-6-0T *Stepney* taking on coal by the stage at New Cross in 1903 soon after renumbering to 655. It was transferred to Brighton the following year after nearly 30 years of service on the South London and East London line suburban services.   *M.P. Bennett/Bluebell Archives*

'Gladstone' class 0-4-2 No. 184 *Carew D. Gilbert*, an Eastbourne engine, stands at its home station. Photographs of this locomotive are none too plentiful with its original name as it was changed to *Stroudley* in September 1906. *M.P. Bennett/Bluebell Archives*

Sister engine No. 195 *Cardew*, seen here at Newhaven, was a regular performer on the night boat train known in the 1890s as the 'Grande Vitesse' service. To ensure that *Cardew* was always manned and ready for duty, the driver was engaged by contract under which the company maintained the engine in good mechanical order and supplied coal, water, oil, grease and cotton waste, whilst the driver was paid a fixed monthly sum and responsible for paying his fireman and a cleaner. To ease *Cardew*'s passage over the curves at Newhaven Harbour the tender was loosely coupled. *E.J. Bedford/John Minnis Collection*

Most enginemen saved a little from their earnings. One driver unfortunately lost his wife after a bad illness, shortly before he retired. It was a bad shock, as he had saved all his life to buy a country 'pub' and had planned to take things easy. However, he was not disappointed. After retiring, he married the barmaid of the local inn, thus getting professional assistance for the country pub which he duly purchased, and lived to the age of ninety-four.

When a new cleaner started work, he was put in a gang, which usually consisted of six boys in charge of a senior cleaner. He was shown how to wipe oil and dirt off the motion. Wheels and paintwork were cleaned with 'patches', which were handfuls of waste soaked in oil. For an extra dirty job, paraffin was added. When wiped off with dry waste, the paintwork 'bobby-dazzled' - the boys' term for a good shine. Splashers, cab sheets, tenders and tank sides were given a coating of tallow, which not only preserved the paint but prevented the dirt from sticking. Tallow only was used on hot boilers, as oil tended to blacken the paint. Powdered bathbrick was used for cleaning brass and copper. After rubbing up a copper chimney top with bathbrick and oil, the boy would put a handful of dry waste down the chimney and make it sooty, then polish the metal with it. The result was a brilliant finish. Some boys with regular engines would spend a penny on a large tin of metal polish, and get an extra finish. These methods still hold good; if my car looks dull after repeated washings, a 'locomotive clean' will make it 'bob' as well as any of the modern car-cleaning preparations.

After 'learning the trade', the boy was given an engine to 'follow', usually a tank engine. He worked either day or night shifts to suit the periods when the engine was in the shed. Shed hours were from 6 am to 5.30 pm with a breakfast break from 8.15 to 9 am, and dinner break from 1 to 2 pm. This applied to both day and night turns, the night shift starting at 6 pm. After tanks, the boys cleaned tender engines, both goods and passenger. It was sometimes necessary for a boy to change from day to night shift during the week, in which case he 'doubled on'; that is, he started at 6 am and knocked off at 4 pm, then came back at 11 pm and carried on until 5.30 am.

The boys were a happy lot, mostly too interested in their work to indulge in horseplay. There was a competition between the boys themselves, and also between different sheds, for turning out the cleanest engines. The boys at Battersea Shed, for example, went so far as to scrub the 'housetops' - that is, cab roofs - with soft soap. These were painted white in those days, to minimise sun heat. The cleaner of No. 184 *Carew D. Gilbert* at Eastbourne Shed, scoured the 'gangway' (running-board or side platforms) bright. The cleaner of No. 195 *Cardew* (which engine always worked the night train) at New Cross Shed, promptly followed suit. Whatever one did, the other did, yet they had never met, and did not even know each others' names!

Chapter Two

Shed Life at New Cross
and Never a Dull Moment

The cleaner boys were a happy crowd, and many folk passing by New Cross depot between 8.30 and 9 pm on most evenings could well confirm that. 'Sounds of music' could be heard issuing from the roundhouse in which the 'Terriers', or 'rooters' as they were usually called, were stabled; this was close to the main road. The 'music' emanated from mouth-organs (nothing so common nowadays - the modern term is 'harmonica') plus two or three flageolet whistles, occasional vocal efforts, and sometimes drum accompaniment provided by banging on the tank sheets of any engine that happened to be within reach.

Don't anyone run away with the idea that this was just hideous cacophony; far from it! Although the mouth-organs were of the kind sold for a shilling or so, most of the boys could get a performance out of them which was not far short of those occasionally heard on present-day radio by crack performers. Half-a-dozen or so made a creditable band, and they knew how to harmonise. So did the flageolet artists. One boy used to play two at once, fixing them together with a couple of elastic bands, and blocking up the three upper holes of one with little pieces of cork. His solo renderings of 'Bluebells of Scotland' (not the Sussex variety!), 'Alice, where art thou' and so on, would have got him a job at the local music hall, had he needed it. When the boys got really warmed up, it sounded better than any so-called modern jazz stuff.

The nickname for the mixture of dirt, ballast dust, oil and grease that accumulated on the engines was 'fass', and naturally the cleaners' nickname was 'fassers'. A boy who had a really musical bent composed a march tune especially suited to mouth-organs, as it had no half-notes, and called it the 'Fassers' March'. It jumped into popularity at once. I recollect the lively tune quite well, and often whistle it unconsciously when busy in my workshop, doing a bit of locomotive building or overhauling.

Life in the sheds was never dull. Something apart from routine was always happening, unexpected, unusual, comic, sometimes tragic. There were also the usual practical jokers to liven things up. One winter morning some crackpot perpetrated a joke which might have had serious results. At one side of the yard was a small shed in which the old chap who put 'pickle' in the tanks, kept his pails and ingredients for making up said 'pickle', which was a kind of water-softening compound. It was just after 6 am and the old man had just lit the tortoise stove which heated the shed. The wood was blazing merrily, when some brainless kite who should have known better, climbed on the roof and dropped several fog-signals down the stovepipe, In a few seconds there was a terrific bang, and the contents of the stove were blown out. The poor old pickle-merchant, scared stiff, dashed across the yard and finished up on the platform of the adjoining station, breathless and almost fainting. The shock was bad enough, but if a train had been coming into the station, the result might easily have been fatal.

There was another old boy whose job it was to clear up the muck that was deposited in the pits after washing out a boiler. On one occasion he had filled his

'E3' class 'Radial' No. 166 *Cliftonville* in goods green livery and shedded at Brighton, pays a visit to Fratton Shed in Portsmouth. *Real Photographs/Ian Allan Ltd*

No. 166 had further lively adventures after the ones described in these pages, receiving a new 'I1' boiler and extended smokebox as the result of an accident in 1918 at East Grinstead while working the 10.55 am Forest Row-Horsted Keynes goods. It is seen here shunting at Crowborough in 1921. *B.C. Vigor/Bluebell Archives*

wheelbarrow with the scale and 'fur', and left it beside the engine while he went to pay an urgent call elsewhere. During his temporary absence, some bright spark jammed a fog-signal under the wheel. When 'Sandy Jack' returned, and lifted the handles of his barrow, it refused to be pushed. Thinking there was a nugget of coal, a clinker, or something similar that was stopping it, he pulled it back a few inches, and then lunged forward. BANG! Over went the barrow, spilling the contents into the pit again. Jack's comments, after recovering, and refilling the 'single-wheeler' were - well, more forcible than polite, shall we say?

Soon after I started work, a 'clever' boilermaker's mate on an engine next to the one I was cleaning, misled by my innocent appearance, asked if I would oblige him by going to the stores and asking for the key of the smokebox. I said 'Certainly', and went off down the shed, tipping off the boys as I passed, to go down to the end if they wanted to see a would-be joker boomeranged. I then took the dart and both handles off the smokebox door of a 'dead' engine, took them to 'Mr Clever', and holding them out, said 'I thought you might like to have the dart and locking handle as well'. The look on his face would have got him a job at Hollywood, if there had been any films in those days, and the roar of laughter from the assembled spectators added to his discomfiture.

One of the 'C' class 0-6-0 Stroudley engines - the most powerful the 'Brighton' possessed at the time, was standing on an otherwise unoccupied shed road, with steam up, waiting for her driver and fireman, about 8.45 one evening. The shed had three roads, with a wall across the end, and on the other side of the wall the roads continued as sidings. On the one level with the engine, there were a dozen wagons loaded with coal. A new boy, seeing that there was no one around, it being evening time, thought he would try his hand at engine-driving, so he got up on the footplate, put her in forward gear, and opened the regulator. The engine moved off, and then the boy apparently found that he could not shut it again, with the result that the engine went clean through the wall and played havoc with the coal wagons. The crash brought the shed staff running to the scene, but the boy disappeared, and nobody saw him again. When 'the bloke' inspected the damage, his comment was 'Well, he might have been a good driver, but he certainly was a damned bad stopper!'

One evening the washout gang had been operating on one of the Billinton radial tanks, and after refilling the boiler, inadvertently left the regulator slightly open. This was not noticed by the firelighter, and the consequence was that as soon as the engine (No. 166 *Cliftonville*) had made sufficient steam to move, she quietly slipped off. By rights, according to rules, the lever should have been in mid-gear, but by the general cussedness of things, it wasn't. Neither was the handbrake screwed on, as the engine had been pushed into the shed by the yard pilot. She moved slowly out of the shed and proceeded down the yard, and nobody took the slightest notice, thinking she was being moved by the shed driver.

The particular line she was on, went down to the end of the yard to a hoist, under which engines were lifted for spring adjustments and so forth. There were no buffer stops, only the boundary fence, and beyond that was the station master's house. The engine just pushed the fence out of the way, and made herself quite at home in the station master's parlour. The wall of the house had to be propped up before she could be pulled out.

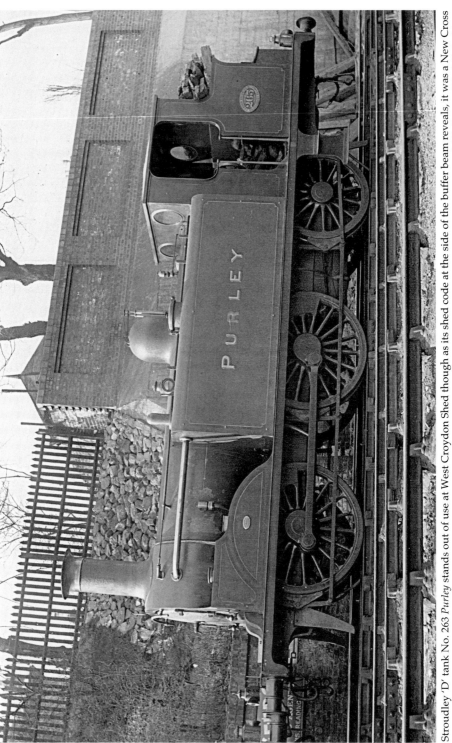

Stroudley 'D' tank No. 263 *Purley* stands out of use at West Croydon Shed though as its shed code at the side of the buffer beam reveals, it was a New Cross engine.

M.P. Bennett/Bluebell Archives

Chapter Three

Incidents on Shed and Misfortunes Never Come Singly

The following anecdote shows that there is apparently some truth in the old adage the 'misfortunes never come singly'! This chapter of accidents took place in the shed at the southern end of the yard at New Cross depot. This shed, known as Croydon Shed, was rather narrow, the footways between the three roads being only a few feet wide, with the washing-out plugholes located at intervals along the centre of each. The plugholes were originally fitted with cast-iron flush fitting covers, but these had long since disappeared, and had not been replaced. In each hole was a big plug cock, the outlet of which was screwed to fit the unions on the washing-out hoses, and the pressure in the water-main to which the cocks were connected was about 100 lb. per square inch. A good pressure was needed to shift the scale and dirt out of the boilers.

The washers-out, who were usually senior cleaners awaiting their turn to be passed for firemen, worked two to a team, and carried their equipment (hoses, spanners, rods, etc.) around the sheds on what was known as a 'whelkstall'. This was a kind of glorified butchers' tray, with handles at each end; and when in transit, the merchant at the leading end would yell out 'Plughole' on approaching one, so that his mate at the trailing end would not literally put his foot in it. Nowadays, the open plugholes would not be tolerated.

Well, one afternoon a cleaner was putting the finishing touches to one of the Stroudley tanks - I think it was No. 263 *Purley* - and she looked a real picture. He was half-lying on the running-board between the front end of the tank and the splasher, with his head and shoulders partly under the boiler barrel, and was wiping the tops of the valve spindles and guide bars, when his bare elbow touched the feed pipe leading from the pump to the side clack on the boiler. Now as bad luck would have it, the side clack was leaking slightly, and the pipe was full of boiling water. Naturally the sudden pain as the cleaner's arm came in contact with the scalding-hot pipe, made him start violently, and he lost his balance and slithered off the running-board. By the general cussedness of things in this benighted world, there chanced to be an open plughole alongside, and the cleaner's foot went down the hole and trod on the handle of the water-cock, pushing it well open. A stream of water immediately shot out, drenching him to the skin, and knocking him off his balance, so that he staggered and fell into the pit in the adjacent road, in which lay a pile of wet and slimy scale that had come from a washed-out engine. Meantime the stream of water, issuing from the cock at high pressure, had reached the rafters of the shed and was fetching down the accumulated soot and dirt of many years, all over the freshly-cleaned engine. You can guess what she looked like!

Fortunately the cleaner was not hurt, but what a sad picture as he arose from the pit, wet through and smothered in chalky scale from head to foot, and contemplated the state of the engine on which he had lavished so much care and labour. A fitter managed to shut the cock by aid of a firebar, and the cleaners' gang was hastily summoned to do the best they could with the engine, which was shortly due out. A fireman who was a member of the St John Ambulance team, took the cleaner into the stores and did the needful for him, so everything came all right in the end. The boy, who saw the funny side of the occurrence after he had got over the shock, was known as 'Unlucky' for months afterwards.

Just after the Boer War ended a party of sailors and marines who had taken part in the battle of Modder River had a 'day out' and were given a civic welcome in London. A special train was arranged for the trip, and as the return journey was routed via New Cross and West Croydon, the staff at the New Cross depot thought it would be a good opportunity to do a bit of 'welcoming' of their own. When the engine came down from London Bridge to the depot to await the time for the return trip, the ringleader tipped off the driver as to what they proposed doing, and got the approximate time that the train would pass the sheds, which adjoined the main line just north of the station. He and a couple of accomplices then went around the sheds and collected all the fog-signals, fire irons, clinker shovels, bells and anything else that could be utilised to kick up a real din.

When the time approached, the officials - who unofficially knew what was in the wind - discreetly got out of the way. Nearly everybody who was on duty at the time, lined up outside the sheds with anything that would make a noise; and after the ordinary train ahead of the special had passed, several of them dashed over to the down main road, and hastily clipped 150 fog-signals to the rails. When the driver of the special, as previously arranged, announced its approach with a 'half-a-pint-of-mild-and-bitter' toot on the whistle, it sounded as if all hell had broken loose. The infernal din practically drowned the noise of the train; and what with the ringing, banging, clattering, hooraying, plus the terrific machine-gun-like rat-tat-tat of the exploding fog-signals, the occupants of the train must have imagined that they were back at Modder River again!

Though far from being a Romany myself, I knew something of gypsy lore, and it once involved me in a tragic occurrence. I booked on for a night goods turn, and found three cleaners and a tube-boy in the engine cab, playing banker with a toy pack of cards, such as could be purchased in those days for a copper or two. They were about the size of cigarette cards. They picked up the cards and got off the engine (it was just at the end of the evening meal break) and were just going away when the tube-boy asked if I would tell his fortune with the cards, as I had done for others, just for amusement. I told him to cut the cards into four parts, and turn them face up, which he did. The combination startled me so much that without realising what I was saying, I told the boy he had less than a fortnight to live. The others laughed, and told him he was unlucky, and no more was thought of it.

Ten days later, when the boy was on the night shift again, he wanted to boil water in a can to make a brew (the nickname for tea) and being unable to find an engine with a clear fire, he thought he would go across to the coaling crane. He was just passing between the buffers of two engines on the coal road, when one of them moved. The driver didn't see him in the dark, and he was caught between the buffers and instantly killed. Coincidence, of course, but you can guess my feelings. From that day to this, I've never told another fortune.

Chapter Four

A Locospotter's Lucky Day
and a Blessing in Disguise

In the days about which I am writing, the term 'engine-spotter' was unknown; but there were plenty of schoolboys who collected the names and numbers of the Brighton engines, and keen competition as to who could compile the biggest list. The children did not haunt the stations, but went to places like Wandsworth Common, and other public places where they could get a good view of passing trains; but occasionally a boy would do his spotting from a station platform. There were no such things as platform tickets in those days, so to gain entry the boy bought a penny ticket to the next station, spent an hour or two on the platform, used his ticket, spent a further period at the next station, and walked back!

One such boy was frequently to be seen at New Cross, and became well known to the station staff. He was well-behaved - rather different from the type of present-day spotter who gets up to so much mischief that British Railways have been compelled to ban them from many stations - and often gave the porters a hand with platform-sweeping, lamp-cleaning and so on. Several times he confided to them that he would love to get into the adjoining locomotive sheds if he could only find a legitimate excuse. Well, it is said that everything comes to those who wait, and one day his chance came.

The line rises from New Cross to Forest Hill (three miles) on a gradient of 1 in 100, and it was the practice to give a push-up-behind with a banking engine to all goods trains longer than about 30 wagons. Any old crock could do this job, as the boiler could be filled and a good fire made up while waiting in the siding, and the 'mighty shove' started under the most favourable conditions. Most drivers also put a 'jimmy' in the blastpipe nozzle, to help an engine in poor shape to steam. This was usually a piece of steel rod cut from a discarded tube-sweeping or washout rod, one end being bent into a hook to clip under the blower union. The rod was laid across the top of the nozzle, and a rail fishplate or similar weight attached to the other end to keep it in place. The effect was to split the jet of exhaust steam and increase the draught on the fire, and was a wonderful help to steaming.

On the day in question, the bank engine was one of Bob Billinton's 0-6-2 tank engines, No. 457 *Watersfield*, one of the earlier series with 4 ft 6 in. wheels, and she was in a pretty bad state, being due for heavy repairs. The driver had made up a sort of 'double jimmy', in the form of a cross, and when the engine made contact with the buffers of the brake van of the train he was assisting, just before reaching New Cross station, he 'gave her the lot' - full gear and full regulator. The blast was so terrific that it dislodged the 'jimmy', and it blew clean out of the chimney as she passed the platform and, as luck would have it, fell a few feet from where the boy was standing. The boy wasn't slow to seize his opportunity to get into the sheds.

There was a pail of water and some cotton waste close by, which had been used for lamp-cleaning. The boy threw the water over the jimmy and fishplate to cool them, then picked up the assembly by help of the waste, took them across to the

'E3' class 0-6-2Ts Nos. 456 *Aldingbourne* (*above*) and 457 *Watersfield*, whose adventures are described in the accompanying pages, were both New Cross engines. They stand in the open area between the Middle and the Croydon Sheds with the palings backing the up local platform immediately behind. *John Minnis Collection and Lens of Sutton*

office in the locomotive yard, and said to the astonished foreman, 'Please, sir, this just fell out of one of your engines!' To his great delight, he was rewarded by permission to look around the sheds. By the way, some years later, blastpipes with a cross cast into the nozzle, similar to the driver's 'double jimmy', were fitted to a number of French locomotives, and the French locomotive engineer got the credit for the improvement in steaming. Great minds often think alike!!

A mishap may sometimes prove a blessing in disguise, and the following is a good instance. One morning we were working a local pick-up goods, another job which any engine in poor fettle could easily manage; the load seldom exceeded 20 wagons (usually less) and longest non-stop run was less than three miles, the furthest point of call being Wimbledon. Our engine was No. 456 *Aldingbourne*, another of the Billinton 4 ft 6 in. radial tanks. She was leaking badly at the tube ends in the firebox, and one injector could barely keep enough steam pressure to run. Luckily the coal was a bit of good Welsh, otherwise we would have been properly sunk.

We pulled into the sidings at East Dulwich to do a spot of shunting, with 80 lb. 'on the clock', and the water in the bottom nut. I took a look in the firebox, and remarked to my mate that the brick arch looked very rocky, and I shouldn't be surprised if it fell down. We dropped two wagons of coal, did the shunting, picked up three empties, blew up to 140 lb. and set off for our next stop, Tulse Hill. Although the load was light, the poor old girl made heavy weather of it, going up Knight's Hill viaduct, and sure enough the heavy blast shook up the rickety brick arch so much that it collapsed just as we got to the tunnel. However, we managed to get to Tulse Hill, pulled into the sidings, and got out the relics of the brick arch with the aid of the clinker shovel.

After doing the usual chores, we had another blow-up and then proceeded to Streatham. I noticed that the water was going up in the glass instead of down, but as we were on a down grade, well notched up, and not using so much steam, I took no notice. Steam had not dropped when we pulled into the sidings, either; so we got busy, did the setting out, shunting, and picking up, and departed for Tooting Junction. Then we both got a shock. The injector was gaining on the boiler, so my mate shut it off, and then - wonder of wonders! - just after passing Streatham Junction South, the old cat started to blow off. We just looked at each other and grinned. Then I guessed what had happened, looked in the firebox again, and found my surmise to be correct. The tubeplate, now directly exposed to the fire, was as dry as a bone.

What happened was that the brick arch had shielded the leaky tube ends from the direct rays of the fire, and the water coming through had prevented the metal from rising above a certain heat. After the arch had collapsed and the remains had been removed, the tube ends were exposed to the direct heat. As I have said, we had a bit of good Welsh coal in the bunker, and the blast when pulling out of Streatham brought the fire up almost to white heat. The effect of this on the tube ends was to expand them, which in turn stopped leakage; so the mishap to the brick arch 'saved our bacon' in a manner of speaking. The rest of the trip was easy as far as maintenance of steam and water was concerned, but care had to be taken to operate the firehole door and avoid cold air blowing on the tubeplate. There are tricks in every trade!

'D' class No. 239 *Patcham,* beautifully turned out, poses with its crew for a photograph at Portsmouth Harbour station. It is in post-1902 condition after receiving a Billinton boiler.

Lens of Sutton

'E4' class No. 500 *Puttenham* receives attention from its fireman while its driver keeps a vigilant eye on the platform side for the right-away to leave Hove. *M.P. Bennett/Bluebell Archives*

Chapter Five

Soft Soap and a Cocky Driver Deflated

There used to be a yarn going around about a driver and fireman who were on their way home one night from the annual dinner of the local branch of the union. The driver had 'filled his gauge-glass over the top nut', and though progress was inclined to be unsteady, he got along fairly well until they approached a doctor's house with the usual red lamp over the gate. On seeing this, the driver stopped, and nothing that his mate could say or do would induce him to proceed. 'No, mate', said he, 'Been carpeted oncesh for running pasht shignal at danger. Ain't goin' on' (pointing to the doctor's lamp) 'till that one turn greenish!'

That was, of course, pure fiction; but here is one that is equally humorous, and absolute fact. One of the Stroudley 'D' class tanks - it was No. 239 *Patcham* if I recollect rightly - had been in for motion repairs, and after the motion work had been re-erected it worked rather stiffly, and required considerable effort to turn the reversing wheel. It was the usual practice to send a tank engine on a shunting job after repairs, to 'work it in', and it so happened that this engine was booked for the night pilot job at Norwood Junction goods yard, normally done by a regular goods tank with a 'pole' reversing lever. Drivers always called a reverser a 'lever', whether it was a long handle working in a notched quadrant, or a wheel-and-screw. By rights an engine with a wheel-and-screw reverser should never have been put on a shunting job which entailed constant reversing; but at the time, it so happened that no other engine was available.

Anyway, the driver did not complain, but managed the night's shunting, and in due course returned to the shed and booked off, just about tired out with operating the stiff reversing gear. Later that morning, the fireman went out to do a bit of shopping, and encountered his mate, looking dejected and miserable. 'Why, Joe', said he, 'you don't half look happy. Anything amiss at home?' 'Only washing-day', replied the driver. 'You know how stiff that —— lever was last night, it damn near wrenched my arm out. Well, no sooner I got inside the house this morning, the missis said "Joe, will you turn the wringer while I put the blankets through it?"'

In Michael Reynolds' book *Engine-Driving Life* there is an account of how a fitter's mate, wanting to play a trick on a 'cocky' driver, put a handful of soft soap in his tender. The soap dissolved, entered the boiler, spread over the firebox and tubes, and caused the engine to stall for want of steam. Many folk have doubted that this could really happen, but I recollect a case where it actually did. The engine was one of the Billinton radial tanks used on passenger work, No. 500 *Puttenham*. One of the cleaners was going to repaint the 'housetop' (cab roof) and it required a good scrubbing to remove the accumulation of soot and grime before the paint could be applied; so he filled his pail from the tank, and then suddenly remembered that he 'had to see a man about a dog', and went off, leaving his pail, a big bunch of waste, and a dollop of soft soap on a piece of brown paper alongside the open tank lid.

The sight of the bunch of waste lying unattended proved too great a temptation for the boy cleaning the adjacent engine, and he decided to snaffle it; but, to avoid being seen, he crouched down as he went along the running-plate, and reached up to grab the waste. In pulling it over toward him, he knocked the paper with the soft soap on it, into the open tank, without knowing what he had done. When the painter returned, and found the waste and soft soap both missing, he naturally concluded that some person unknown had snaffled the lot. Calling down blessings upon the head of the culprit, he went off to the stores and obtained a fresh supply, and finished his job.

Nobody suspected that the soap had gone into the tank until the engine failed for steam when it went out on its next turn of duty. As the water in the gauge glasses looked cloudy and frothy, the boiler was emptied, and the trouble came to light. The boy who had been cleaning the next engine, when questioned, admitted sneaking the bundle of waste, but stoutly denied putting the soap into the tank. When the paper was found in the tank, it was plain to see what had happened.

I mentioned 'cocky' drivers. Well, there was one at New Cross depot who was always boasting about his knowledge of locomotives in general, his ability to handle any engine, and his scorn of any driver who lost time because the engine was in poor condition. It was common knowledge that he always ran with a 'jimmy' in the blastpipe nozzle of his own engine, and used more coal than most other engines of the same class (small boiler 4-4-0). He tipped the shop blacksmith to make a special 'jimmy', which had two projections fitting into the blast nozzle and which were tightened by a wing nut, so that instant insertion and removal were possible.

It so happened that his engine was booked for the station master's annual excursion, and for this job the engines were always decorated with garlands of artificial flowers, an ornamental edging around the cab roof, a shield with the company's coats-of-arms on the smokebox door, and various other embellishments. On the morning of the trip, 'Mr Cocky' found to his great dismay that the shield prevented him from opening the smokebox door and inserting his jimmy in the blast nozzle. Nearly everybody in the sheds predicted what was going to happen, and sure enough it did - the engine 'stuck for steam' before the train reached Forest Hill, and an old goods engine (the only engine available) had to be sent out to replace the dolled-up cripple. It is hardly necessary to add that such a showdown evaporated much of the driver's cockiness!

It came to pass that the children of Israel who dwelt in the land of Bethnal Green that is beyond Shoreditch, yearned for a day at the seaside, and pooled their shekels for a special from Shoreditch to Brighton. As a big tender engine would not clear the load gauge of the East London line, it was arranged that a 'Terrier' would pull the train from Shoreditch to New Cross, and the main line engine would take it from there to Brighton. As Bobby Burrrrrns remarked, 'the best-laid plans o' mice and men gang aft agley', and through some misunderstanding there was no tender engine waiting to take the special when it arrived at New Cross.

The driver of the 'Terrier', No. 50 *Whitechapel* (I believe it was George Gore, who afterwards drove *Cardew* regularly on the Newhaven night boat train) promptly volunteered to carry on with the job, and after filling up his tanks, proceeded to demonstrate what one of Billy Stroudley's babies could do. The load was 11 or 12 four-wheelers - 'workmen's thirds' - packed to capacity, and from the standing start, the tiny engine accelerated up the 1 in 100 and passed Forest Hill, blowing off, in fine style. She stopped at East Croydon for another drink, then set her back into it again up the 1 in 264 to Merstham Tunnel, after which she ran like a deer with another stop at Three Bridges for more water. On the down grades she knocked off a mile per minute (the driver said she must have been doing all of 70 mph through Haywards Heath) and arrived at Brighton 8 minutes late, all of which was accounted for by the water stops. The return trip was made in similar vigorous fashion; maybe the little engine enjoyed her day out from the East London tunnels! This episode took place over 60 years ago - and people talk about 'modernisation', diesels, and so on!

'Terrier' *Whitechapel*, numbered 650 in the Duplicate List in 1901, stands with its crew beside the Croydon Shed at New Cross whence it frequently visited its namesake via the Thames Tunnel on East London line services. This locomotive survives today on the preserved Kent and East Sussex Railway having commandeered the name of *Sutton* from another member of the class.   *Lens of Sutton*

Chapter Six

Footplate Life and All the Tricks of the Trade

Footplate life on the old 'Brighton' around the turn of the century was far different from what it is at the present time. Though sometimes the hours were long, and the work hard, nobody seemed to worry; there was always plenty of interest. Billy Stroudley's dictum of 'one driver, one engine' was adhered to as much as possible. Billy said that it kept maintenance costs to rock bottom, and he certainly was right. It stands to reason that with 'Jack Robinson, driver' painted up inside his cab for all to see, Jack had some cause to be proud of his iron horse, and looked after it well. Nowadays, under the 'common user' system, nobody cares a bean. Drivers and firemen booked on an hour before train time, and got their engines ready. They would not leave the shed unless they knew she was right. Consequently, failures on the road were few and far between. How different from the so-called 'modern' way of working!

Doing a night's shunting at Willow Walk, Norwood Junction or some other goods depot, was inclined to be monotonous, but on the road things sometimes got a bit hectic. It certainly gave the lie to the old saying about more haste, less speed. For example, take the passenger tank jobs during the evening peak rush. Many of the outer suburban trains from London Bridge made Norwood Junction the first stop, and some of the timings were pretty tight, needing quite a bit of good enginemanship. To keep time and allow for the passengers getting off entailed a start-to-stop run of 13 minutes for a shade over nine miles, which included the three-mile 1 in 100 bank from New Cross to Forest Hill. This would be praiseworthy for modern emu stock, or a BR 2-6-4 tank engine with a moderate load; but the little Stroudley 'D' class tanks used to do it regularly with a seven-coach bogie set, plus one or two spares, crowded to capacity with straphangers in every compartment, and all the springs out straight!

A good start was half the battle, so when backing on to the train the trick was to open the trailing sands (unless the rails were exceptionally dry) and sand the rails from the last pair of points back to the train. If anybody dropped sand actually *in* the points they stood a good chance of being stuck up against the fence and shot at dawn, or something equally pleasant! The engine wheels rolled down the sand into a fair imitation of a macadam road, on which it was next to impossible to slip. Consequently, on getting the 'right-away', the regulator could be pushed about three parts open; and if the engine was blowing off, as she usually was, she would dig her heels in, give one mighty heave and off we would go. It was advisable to hold the regulator handle as she threaded her way through the points and crossings outside the station, in case she lost her feet; but as soon as the last one was safely negotiated, over went the regulator to full open and the reversing wheel brought back to about 45 per cent cut-off. The acceleration was something really worth writing home about!

Starting like this, a modern engine would try to blow the chimney off the smokebox; not so our little darlings, as part of the exhaust steam went into the tanks and warmed up the feedwater. However, the blast was sharp enough to make the fire step lively, so the fireman popped in a few shovelfuls of black diamonds around the sides of the firebox and under the door, as she steamed best with a 'saucer' fire. On went one pump, and as soon as the fresh coal caught alight, on went the other, unless the water was up in the top nut of the water-gauge. They steamed best with about three-parts of a glass. Meantime the high rate of acceleration continued, and by the time we passed Blue Anchor Junction - Corbet's Lane, where the South Eastern and South London lines diverged - we were doing the best part of a mile a minute. The reverser could then be brought back a little more.

Faster and faster we went, in order to 'rush the bank', until the wheels were turning so quickly that the coupling-rods were hardly visible as we whizzed through New Cross and hit the bottom of the long climb. As the engine felt the drag of the load behind her tail, she slowed a little; then the cut-off could be advanced until she settled down to a steady pull. Most drivers could 'sense' the position of the reverser at which she developed her maximum power. Speed would not fall any further, and up she would go, both pumps feeding, the fire nearly white, safety-valves on the sizzle, and the exhaust beats perfectly even, though so rapid that they sounded like the purr of an outsize cat. It did not need much imagination to hear her give a sigh of relief as she passed Forest Hill, then she would 'gather her skirt' and race down through Sydenham, Penge and Anerley for all she was worth. Steam could be shut off just after passing Anerley; then approaching the crossing from main to local at Norwood Jn a slight brake application would check her frantic dash sufficiently to allow her to negotiate the crossover safely. Then a carefully-timed final application would bring her to rest right opposite the water-crane near the end of the down local platform well on time.

While the passengers were getting off, the fireman would climb on the tank top and put the crane hose in the filling hole, while the driver manipulated the water valve, to give the engine a well-earned drink. She needed it! The race against the clock would nearly empty the tanks; plenty of steam needs plenty of water. Incidentally, it often puzzled passengers how the driver could stop exactly in the right place for the crane hose to reach the filler. Well, that was just another trick of the trade; a tribute both to the Westinghouse air brake and to the Stroudley brake valve. It was possible to make a chalk mark on the platform, and another on the engine's running-board, and with two brake applications, pull up with the chalk marks within a few inches of each other, even from full speed. After filling up, the journey to Stoats Nest (later Coulsdon North), West Croydon, Sutton, Epsom or wherever it might be was resumed at a little more leisurely speed, though the timings were only slightly below those of the present day electric trains.

Speaking of tricks of the trade, the orders were that suburban trains were always to stop with the first-class compartments nearest to the ticket barriers, so that first-class passengers would have the least distance to walk when alighting from trains. As the first-class compartments were always in the middle of the suburban train sets, this was an easy job when the engine was running chimney first, as the driver would be on the platform side of the engine, and could gauge the stop nicely. However, when running bunker first, with the driver on the side away from the platform, it was not so easy, so what we did was to note an advertisement, or other 'landmark', on the opposite platform, and stop with the engine opposite to it.

There was a catch in this, however, because engine-drivers, like other human beings, cannot remember everything; and it sometimes came to pass that a driver got the stations mixed, and stopped at 'Beecham's Pills' when he should have stopped at 'Bovril'. The usual result was that some pompous old buffer, maybe a shareholder in the company, had to walk a few more steps from the carriage to the ticket barrier, and promptly wrote a letter of complaint to the General Manager!

There were three classes of carriages in those days - first, second and third, and the railwaymen had an amusing definition of the passengers who rode in them. First-class passengers, they said, were 'toffs'; third-class passengers were ordinary common people; but second-class passengers were ordinary common people who wanted to make believe they were 'toffs'!

Lawson Billinton's 'Baltic' 4-6-4T No. 332 'sprints up hill' on Forest Hill Bank near Honor Oak Park in 1926 in charge of the down 'City Limited' which contains a Pullman car in the middle of its formation. (*See page 49.*)   *O.J. Morris/Lens of Sutton*

Chapter Seven

Timekeeping Problems

The Stroudley engines were better than the Billinton engines in several ways. They were much livelier, could get away quicker and run like deer; they also steamed freely. It was a standing joke that a Stroudley engine would make steam with a torchlamp on top of the brick arch! On the other hand, the Billinton engines were sluggish, slow to accelerate and seemed to have a definite maximum speed above which they would not run. If we tried to force them, they seemed to choke themselves, and could not get rid of the exhaust steam. As I have mentioned part of the Stroudley engines' exhaust went into the tanks and warmed the feedwater, but as the Billinton engines all had injectors which would not feed hot water, all the exhaust was forced to go out of the chimney. Steam from the boiler had, of course, to be used for working the injectors.

The difference in performance was due to the different arrangement of steam and exhaust ports, slide valves, and valve settings. Regular passengers soon discerned that the engines with copper tops to the chimneys were livelier and faster than those with plain black cast-iron chimneys, and an amusing instance of this took place one evening at London Bridge during the evening rush period. With the intensive suburban services both on the LB&SCR and the South Eastern it was inevitable that some of the departure times from London Bridge should be the same. Although it was 'against the rules', human nature being what it is, it was also inevitable that when a Brighton and a South Eastern train found themselves neck-and-neck just after leaving their respective stations, the drivers just could not resist having a friendly dust-up as far as South Bermondsey (Corbet's Lane) where the tracks diverged. The South Eastern engines were mostly trailing bogie tanks (0-4-4) of Jimmy Stirling's design, with an occasional gaily-painted Wainwright of the same type. The regular passengers shared in the excitement, and bets were frequently placed as to which train would reach the winning-post (junction signals) first.

Enginemen soon recognised regular passengers, naturally, and several of them particularly noticed a ginger-headed Irishman who would come up and take a look at the engine, and pass a cheery greeting. One evening a driver, feeling curious as to why Pat always came to see the engine, asked him if he was interested in them. Pat's reply was distinctly illuminating. Said he, 'Shure Oi am an' all! The bhoys in our carriage bets on whether ye'll lick the South Eastern train down to Bermondsey, so Oi comes and looks at the ingin. If she's got a copper top, Oi bets on the Brighton train. If she hasn't, Oi bets on the South Eastern - an' Oi always wins!' The prosperous City folk who were first-class season-ticket holders and travelled on the 5 pm London Bridge to Brighton held the same views as Pat, and were not slow to express them. When the Billinton 4-4-0s first came out, one was tried on the 'Stockbrokers' Limited' as it was jocularly known, but just could not handle it, losing time

'E4' Radial' No. 506 *Catherington* stands on the New Cross turntable in 1903. Several of this class saw service across the Channel in France during World War I.   *M.P. Bennett/Bluebell Archives*

'E1' class 0-6-0T No. 149 *Lucerne* outside Brighton Paint Shops in 1909, as its newly conditioned wheels and coupling rods indicate. But the chimney and smokebox clearly show the effects of a period in store outdoors at Horsted Keynes. *Lucerne* had a steam trial before being repainted and losing its name but nevertheless retained its Stroudley characteristics. It also exchanged depots, severing its connection with New Cross and moving to West Croydon.

Ralph Stent Collection

badly on every trip. The passengers, many of whom were shareholders, 'big noises' in the City, and friends of the Directors, kicked up such a shindy that orders went forth that no more Billinton engines were to be put on the train, and it was always hauled by one of Stroudley's 'Gladstone' class. These engines had no difficulty in keeping time.

Incidentally many years after, when the 'Gladstones' had all gone to the locomotive Valhalla, one of the big 4-6-4 tank engines did a wonderful job of work one evening on the same train. Due to some mishap which had upset the traffic, No. 332 was delayed by signals, and passed East Croydon nine minutes late. Then she got a clear road, and proceeded to knock off the arrears with such vigour that she arrived at Brighton on time, 40 miles in 36 minutes. The load was 10 first-class bogie coaches plus Pullman car *Anaconda*. The big cylinders - 22 in. x 28 in. - enabled her to sprint uphill!

Some of the drivers of the Billinton radial tanks (0-6-2) became rather fed up with continual reports about running late. They knew what was the cause of the poor acceleration and 'so-fast-and-no-faster' running, and decided to do something about it, so got on to their district superintendents and suggested improving the valve gear and setting. The DS's reply was that this was a question for Mr Billinton to deal with, as they had no power to alter any part of the design of the engines. They suggested that the best thing to do, was for a senior driver from each shed to form a deputation, go down to Brighton and see the boss, and put their suggestions before him. This was done, but the result was not exactly as anticipated! Poor old Bob suffered from cancer (it got him in the end, in 1904) and it made him rather irascible at times. It so happened that on the day the deputation went down, he was properly out of sorts, and consequently not in the best of tempers. Pressure rose steadily while the drivers were putting their case and making their suggestions; and when they had finished, he just 'blew off'. He told the drivers that there was nothing the matter at all with the engines. All they needed was correct handling; the drivers were nothing more than a pack of semi-skilled labourers with no knowledge of how to run the engines properly, and so on for about 10 minutes, after which he ordered the deputation out of his office.

The crestfallen drivers returned to their depots and reported results to their superintendents; after consultations, it was decided to try and improve the engines *sub rosa*. Exhaust cavities in the valves were lengthened, eccentrics reset to give better valve events, and other improvements made which enabled the engines to run much more freely; and the old trouble of eccentric-straps running hot disappeared. If old Bob ever found out, he made no comment; the drivers, learning the cause of his rudeness, freely forgave him, so all ended happily.

The Russians reckoned that they were the first to put a space satellite into orbit, but they were not the first to try - not by long chalks! One of the radial tanks, No. 506 *Catherington*, had a darned good shot at it one Sunday afternoon in 1902. She was one of the earlier series that had the Stroudley type of spring-balance safety valves mounted on the dome. She was working the 4.30 pm London Bridge to Victoria via Norwood Junction and Selhurst, due at New Cross at 4.37 pm. I was on shed duty that afternoon, and saw her approaching on the down local line, slowing down for the stop, when suddenly there was a terrific roar, and a tremendous cloud of steam shot from the dome, like the pictures you see of an atom bomb going off. She managed to get to the platform, where the steam died down, and then we saw what had happened. One of the safety valve levers had broken off close to the eye by which it was attached to the spring column, and swung right back, while the valve itself had disappeared into space, releasing the steam, which had blown out and taken most of the water with it.

We took out the yard pilot, the 'Terrier' *Surrey*, and pulled the unfortunate 'Cathie' off the train. Being a Sunday afternoon, there was only one engine in steam in the yard, one of the old 'black tanks' (Stroudley 'E' class 0-6-0) No. 149 *Lucerne*, to the best of my recollection, and she was hastily requisitioned to take on the train. It did not take long to fix up 'Cathie' with a fresh balance lever and valve, and get her in steam again. We later discovered the old valve never went into orbit, after all, as it was found in the yard of the Mazawattee Tea warehouse in a side street some distance from the station a few days after the occurrence.

Billinton 'Grasshopper' 4-4-0 No. 203 *Henry Fletcher* entering Ashstead LSWR station on the section between Leatherhead and Epsom, over which the LB&SCR had running powers. *M.P. Bennett/Bluebell Archives*

Chapter Eight

Bob Billinton's 'Grasshoppers' and Some Free Dinners

Although Bob Billinton's 4-4-0 'Grasshoppers' were barred from the 5 pm, London Bridge to Brighton, one of them always worked the Sunday 'Pullman Limited' (Bob saw to that!) and as this train was only a light one, they usually managed to scrape in on time. It was, however, a sore point with the drivers of the Stroudley 'Gladstones' at Battersea Shed that they never got a chance to show what they could do with the same load. At that time it consisted of three or four Pullman cars, with a Pullman 'pup' at each end. The 'pups' were just passenger brake vans dolled up to look like Pullman cars, to match those in the train, and contained a big dynamo, belt-driven from one of the axles, and a set of accumulators for the lights in the cars. I believe the 'Brighton' was a pioneer of electric train-lighting. As I mentioned before, everything comes to those who wait; and one Sunday morning, the long-wished-for opportunity presented itself.

Most of Bob's engines suffered from leaky tubes. I remember George Sargent, who drove No. 203 *Henry Fletcher* out of New Cross depot, and who was always at the bottom of the coal premium list (his usual average was around 60 lb. per mile) telling 'the bloke' that he could do much better if his engine would only burn water. The engine booked to take the Pullman train that morning, No. 213 *Bessemer*, the one with the larger boiler - was leaking so badly that the driver told the shed foremen that she would not be able to manage the job. A lot of publicity had been given to this train and, as late running would have made a serious blot in the LB&SCR copybook, it presented a problem. Then the shed foreman had a brainwave. The only other engine in steam was a 'Gladstone', No. 187 *Philip Rose*, booked for a National Sunday League cheap excursion to Brighton. He suggested that the engines should swap trains, and the driver of No. 187 (Jack Pullen, if memory serves rightly) agreed with alacrity, as it was the very thing he had been waiting for. 'Bessie's' driver said he didn't mind, as it didn't matter about losing time with the trippers.

Meantime, the clock was doing its non-stop run, and the station master at Victoria was all in a tizzy about the non-appearance of the engine for the Pullman. When it eventually appeared and matters were explained, he asked the driver to get a move on, so as to avoid breaking faith with the passengers. Old Jack just smiled and said he would do his best. He certainly did! It was around 11.13 when he got the 'right-away'. He reckoned he passed East Croydon about eleven minutes later, maintained well over the mile-a-minute up to Merstham tunnel, and then went up into the nineties, finally landing at Brighton right on the dot. There was not much water left in the tender. The fireman said he thought they would have to shut off at Hassocks, to avoid running down Brighton Pier and finishing up in the Channel.

When old Bob heard of it he nearly blew his top, and carpeted the driver for running at excessive speed, telling him that if there had been a pitch-in, he would have been charged with manslaughter. The driver said no, he wouldn't,

The unique 'B3' class representative No. 213 *Bessemer* passes Balham Intermediate signal box leading a cavalcade of 16 vehicles, mainly of Stroudley vintage including the interesting old Brighton luggage van at the front. *Bessemer* emerged from Brighton Works in January 1898 and was a 'B2' to all intents and purposes but with a much larger boiler. When Earle Marsh became locomotive superintendent he gave it the 'B3' classification. The 'double diamond' disc suggests a holiday or excursion special.   *Dr T.S. Budden*

In November 1908 *Bessemer* was converted to class 'B2X' fitted with a Marsh 'C3' boiler, and is seen here emerging with the 'Continental Express' from Lewes Tunnel.
                                                           M.P. Bennett/Bluebell Archives

'Gladstone' class 0-4-2 No. 187 *Philip Rose* rests in the centre road at East Croydon between turns of duty. Many of the 'Gladstones' were named after Directors, often still currently serving on the Board of the London Brighton and South Coast Railway. *Lens of Sutton*

Record breaking 'Scotchman' No. 70, so called because the majority of the 'B4' class were built north of the border by Sharp, Stewart & Co., stands at the north end of East Croydon station. *Holyrood* on 26th July, 1903 ran from Victoria to Brighton in 48 minutes 41 seconds at an average of 63.4 mph. *Lens of Sutton*

as he would have been killed, but he only had one neck and knew how to look after it. There was an 'unwritten law' that if the boss used unparliamentary language, he could be answered in the same strain, and 'nothing done" and they went hammer-and-tongs for 15 minutes or so. Finally Bob gave the driver a few days' suspension 'to cool him off a bit', but the driver had the last word. As he was leaving the office, he turned around and told Bob that there was a damned sight more 'go' in *Philip Rose*'s tender than in any Billinton engine! Many years after, John Tompsett, driving No. 70 *Holyrood*, one of the bigger 4-4-0 Billinton engines, made an 'official' run with a light load, and a specially-cleared road, to see how quickly the trip could be knocked off; but his time (I have forgotten exactly what it was) did not beat the Stroudley engine's timing.

Incidentally, I often wonder what a 'modernised' Stroudley engine could do. I have a 3½ in. gauge *Grosvenor* (one-sixteenth of full size) and when building her, I incorporated all 'mod cons' such as long-travel valves, high superheat, mechanical lubrication, and so forth. My weight on a bogie car is equal to 320 ton train, but she treats it like a bag of feathers, and has run over 1½ actual miles on one firing, at a speed equivalent to nearly 80 mph, the exhaust beats being almost inaudible. On that showing, the full-size engine, with a 250 lb. superheater boiler, 20 in. piston-valve cylinders, and long-travel valves with my pet setting, should be able to run the 'Brighton Belle' in 45 minutes or less. Old as I am, I'd love to try it! Readers may have seen my little railway, just south of Purley Oaks station, on the up side. It can easily be located by the full-size LB&SCR signal which came from Coulsdon North station, and which I converted to automatic working. I have 18 locomotives, including a small edition of a GWR 10 ft 'single' built in 1838, and an LNWR three-cylinder Webb compound. They are all 'goers'!

The mention of hunting usually calls to mind red coats, horses, hounds, foxes, tally-ho and what-have-you. It will come as a surprise to many that hunting can be done from a locomotive footplate. Around the turn of the century, the railway banks near Haywards Heath were honeycombed with rabbit burrows, and the bunnies became so used to passing trains that they took no notice of them, running about on the banks in full view. It frequently happened that the driver or fireman of a goods train, or a passenger train slowing down or stopping for a signal, took a pot-shot at one with a nugget of coal, and usually scored a bull's-eye, which often as not finished bunny's earthly career. A big lump of coal hurled with considerable force from a moving engine was something to be reckoned with.

In that event, the engineman would write the number of his engine, and the approximate time he would pass the station on the return trip, on a piece of paper, wrap a small piece of coal in it, and throw it on the station platform, with a toot on the whistle. A porter would then go along the bank, retrieve the defunct bunny, and throw it on the tender as the engine passed on the return trip. It is hardly necessary to add that the driver slowed down for the purpose! Some of the crews became expert shots, and provided the station staff with quite a few Sunday dinners, as well as their own. Tell it not in Gath, but there were rumours that more than one home fire was kept burning with the lumps of coal that were retrieved along with the rabbits.

I got mixed up in a hunt of another kind one night. We were just south of Earlswood station, and going at a tidy clip, when, looking over the side of the cab, I saw something moving on the line ahead. We were over it before you could say Bill Bailey. My heart jumped up into my throat, I thought it was somebody committing suicide and told my mate. He only laughed, and said I was imagining things. However, I could not rest, and when we stopped at Lewes I got down and investigated. The 'suicide' was a sheep. How it got on the line I don't know, but the front of the engine was in a shocking mess with the remains of it. When we got to the end of the trip, we managed to recover enough undamaged mutton for a couple of good dinners. The occurrence was duly reported, but where the unfortunate animal came from remained a mystery, for no farmer ever put in a claim.

'B4' class 4-4-0 No. 70 at Eastbourne, whence it was transferred in 1905 from Brighton, appropriately receiving the name of *Devonshire*, a noble family closely associated with that resort through its local landholdings. The crew give their locomotive a final going over prior to departure with a northbound express.   *M.P. Bennett/Bluebell Archives*

'D' tank No. 235 *Broadwater* received a variety of shed allocations during its days on the Brighton. In the mid-Edwardian period it was based at Horsham, but is seen here ready for the return trip from Portsmouth Harbour via the Mid-Sussex line. Note the blistered paintwork on the chimney and smokebox.

Lens of Sutton

Chapter Nine

The Coal Premium List
and the Sad Case of 'Nuts'

I mentioned earlier a New Cross driver who was always at the bottom of the coal premium list; and maybe for the benefit of the uninitiated, I had better explain what this was. Drivers were not only encouraged to look after their engines, but to run them as economically as possible, and to that end they were paid a premium for the coal they saved from the usual allowance. On the passenger engines, this was 17 lb. per mile for the engine, and 1¼ lb. for every four wheeled coach. A six-wheeler counted as 1½, and a bogie coach as two four-wheelers, a special allowance being made for stock such as 12-wheeled Pullman cars. The premium was one penny per cwt. for all coal not used. It does not sound much at today's distorted values, but the enginemen managed to make a good thing out of it, both to their own and the company's advantage. It was no uncommon occurrence for a driver and fireman to share 30s. per month 'coal money' as they called it; and in those days, when 'fags' were five a penny, and a pint of 'wallop' cost twopence, the extra cash was a welcome addition to their ordinary wages. One young fireman, on receiving his first payment, remarked 'Gorlummy, looks as though the less coal we shovel the more we get paid for it!'

A list was put up at each shed every month, giving the drivers' names and the amount of coal consumed. A small minority of the drivers did not worry, and as long as they got along all right, and kept time, coal consumption was a secondary consideration. However, some drivers got up to all sorts of antics to keep near the top of the list. Lay folk would be surprised to know the difference that skilled driving and firing can make to the amount of coal that an engine will burn; but as I remarked before, there are tricks in every trade and one driver made use of a perfectly legitimate trick that not only kept him at the top of the coal list, but presented the Locomotive Department with a problem that defied all their efforts to solve.

His engine was No. 235 *Broadwater*, a Stroudley 'D' class tank, at Tunbridge Wells Shed and, according to the coal consumption records, she only needed enough black diamonds to keep herself going, pulling her trains without any extra at all. She kept time all right, needed no more maintaining than any of her sisters, and did not appear to differ from them in any respect whatever; but there it was. She was doing the job on 10 lb. or more per mile below the average for the whole class - *but how?* In an endeavour to find out, she was taken to Brighton Works, pulled all to pieces, and every component carefully examined to see if it differed from standard construction. It didn't! She was tried on two or three local trips, and her coal consumption appeared to be normal; but as soon as she returned to Tunbridge Wells, she became the frugal Scotswoman again. Incidentally, she was built by Neilson's of Glasgow, the firm which supplied the LB&SCR with a number of the 'D' class tanks to Stroudley's drawings.

Anyway, they gave it up, and the mystery was never solved until the driver eventually went on main line work with a tender engine at another shed and then he spilled the beans. Coal was loaded into bunkers and tenders direct from coal wagons on a line adjoining the 'coal road', by a small steam crane and skips, or 'tubs' as they were usually called. The crane dropped the tub into a wagon, where the 'coalies' filled it, and the crane then hoisted it over the bunker or tender. Another 'coalie' 'pulled the string', which allowed the bottom of the tub to open, and the contents dropped out. Naturally not every nugget reached its intended destination; some was inevitably spilled on to the ballast. This was swept up at intervals, and put into a spare tub; but there was always a certain amount of stones, ballast and dirt swept up with it, and it would have hardly been fair to put this into the engine bunkers or tenders and count it as part of the allowance. At the same time, it would have been sheer waste to throw it away, and to sort out the coal from the sweepings by hand would have been decidedly an uneconomic proposition.

To avoid wasting, any driver who cared to take a 'tub of muck', as it was usually known, along with his coal allowance, did not have it booked up to him. With a good free-steaming engine, the coal in the 'muck' burned up as usual, while the stuff that would not burn either went through the bars into the ashpan or formed clinkers easily removed after the day's run. In any case, as the tubs held 10 cwt. the engine crew were tenpence in pocket. What the driver of *Broadwater* did, was to tip the 'coalies' to save him all the 'muck', and as she was a first-class steamer, she just burnt it up along with the ordinary coal and it made enough steam to pull her train. Two tubs of coal and one of 'muck' put 1½ tons of fuel into the engine's bunker, but only one ton was booked to the driver. That explained the presence of 'the milk in the coconut'; it was perfectly legitimate, but it speaks volumes for the efficiency of the engine and the skill of her crew. George Gore, who ran the night boat train from London Bridge to Newhaven for many years with No. 195 *Cardew* ('Gladstone' class) was also a dab hand at getting along on a proportion of 'muck', but not to the same extent as his fellow-conspirator at Tunbridge Wells.

Strange characters are to be found in every organisation, and the LB&SCR was no exception. One of the strangest that I ever met was the cleaners' foreman at New Cross at the turn of the century. He was a bearded man of medium height and build, John Caplen by name, and a more unfitted man to be a foreman it would be hard to imagine. The boys called him 'Nuts' and he certainly looked and acted 'nutty', yet somehow I rather liked him. Rumour had it that he got the job in return for some service to the company during an unofficial strike. He had a peculiar way of adding 's' to many words when talking. He was known all over the Brighton system; one of the first things I remember about Hastings Shed was a crude sketch of a heart with an arrow through it, done in red chalk on one of the doors, and under it the words 'Nuts of New Cross is doomed'. Personally I hadn't the heart to make fun of him, and if I encountered him in the sheds I just gave him a cheery 'good morning' or whatever it happened to be.

One afternoon I had just booked on, and was doing the usual chores before going out, when he came down the shed, stopped by the engine, and called to me. 'Just looks at thats', he said. 'Thats', as he called it, was 'NUTS' in letters over a foot high, scoured out in bathbrick in the grime on one of the 'E' class tanks standing on the adjacent road. The paint had gone black through lack of cleaning (the goods tanks did not get cleaned very often, they were always working) and the letters stood out in the undercoat. 'It's a shame, Jack', I replied. He looked at me pathetically for a moment, and then said 'Looks, you're a good sorts, you don't guys old Jacks. If you sees thats anywheres and gets a chance to rubs it outs, you'll do it, won't yers?' I said I certainly would. Just then a well-aimed wet socker sailed over the engine and knocked his bowler hat off. He hastily retrieved it, and hurried off, muttering 'The young ————-s, waits till I catches 'em!' Some foreman!

A change in superintendency speedily saw the end of Jack's railway service. The last I saw of him was some years after, when on my way home one evening. He was standing at a street corner, looking very down-and-out. His face lighted up when I stopped and spoke to him. He told me he had been out of work for a long time, but was trying to earn a crust as a doorstep salesman, and offered me a packet of tea, saying 'Would you buys thats off old Jacks, for old times sake, it'll make a few brews'. I gave him a few coppers, shook his hand and hastily turned away - I couldn't keep the tears back. I heard not long afterwards that he had passed on. It takes all sorts to make a world; life is like that!

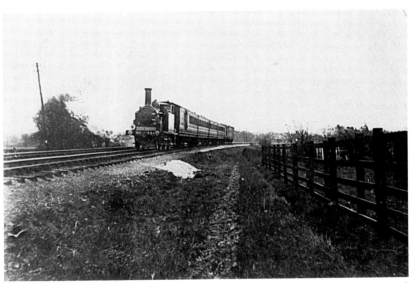

This photograph was on the reverse side of the Great Invitation (*illustrated on page 6*) and shows Stroudley class 'D' 0-4-2T No. 351 *Chailey* on a local train.

This interesting photograph of 'Single' No. 348 *Lullington* was taken outside the shed entrance at Littlehampton, having worked down a Sunday School excursion. The analysis of the headcode is as follows: the 'collar' in front of the chimney denotes working via the Quarry line, the 'double diamonds' a special, the white and 'hot cross bun' discs London Bridge to Littlehampton. The disconnected loose Westinghouse hose at the front indicates that it has already towed out another lot of empty stock, so No. 348 must have been on the first of more than one 'Treat' special. The Westinghouse brake hose was never a feature of Stroudley's time, for he maintained that his passenger engines should never haul tender first.

Lens of Sutton

Chapter Ten

The 'Influence of Drink'

Reading in the paper the other day about a motorist summoned for driving under the influence of drink reminded me of an incident which happened around the turn of the century. I mentioned previously that the Brighton enginemen were never afraid of work, and big pay tickets were the order of the day, especially during the holiday periods. A driver who had been off duty owing to a short illness, and had only been on the job again for a few days, was on his way to the sheds one evening to work a night Portsmouth goods train, when he began to feel rather shaky. Knowing that drivers were what bureaucrats are pleased to call 'in short supply', and not wishing to put 'the bloke' to the trouble of finding a substitute at short notice, he thought that maybe he could carry on if he took a stimulant; so he called in at the next 'pub' and took a small tot of brandy. This seemed to have the desired effect; he felt better, went on, got his engine ready, took her to Willow Walk, picked up his load, and started out for Portsmouth.

For some reason I have long forgotten he did not have his regular fireman that night, but instead had a young fireman who had not long been passed. This man was a quiet sort of chap who had collected the reputation of being 'religious', because he did not speak the kind of 'railroad Esperanto' commonly in use, carefully avoiding unparliamentary expressions in his conversation. I knew him well, and he told me that it was just because he was a bit absentminded, and if he inadvertently loosed off a few shed adjectives at home, it would distress his old mum and dad, who were very prim and proper, so he avoided them altogether. Not a bad wheeze, when you come to think of it!

Anyway, everything went according to routine until the train had passed Sutton, when the driver began to feel poorly again. He tried to pull himself together, but to no purpose - you can't defy nature and get away with it - and between Cheam and Ewell he staggered across the footplate, collapsed on the seatbox, and fainted. The alarmed fireman grabbed him to prevent him from resting against the hot boiler backhead, and in doing so, got a whiff of his breath, in which a trace of the brandy still remained. The fireman immediately jumped to the conclusion that his mate had had 'one over the eight', and would probably pull round; and not wishing to get him into any trouble by stopping and getting assistance, which would also have caused delay to traffic, he decided to try and carry on for a bit, which might give the driver a chance to recover.

As luck would have it, the engine was one of the later series of Billinton 'Vulcans', then being delivered by the Vulcan Foundry, only a few months old, and in good fettle. She was pulling a tidy load - the Portsmouth goods frequently loaded up to 60 wagons and a brake van - and the train usually had a clear road. As soon as the fireman saw that the distant signal at the beginning of each section was showing green, he knew he was all right to do his firing and work the injectors as required, and got along in fine style. The one-man job plodded steadily along, through Epsom and Dorking, but the driver had shown no sign of recovering consciousness, and the fireman was beginning to wonder what he should do about it, when fate took a hand. Somebody on one of the stations had seen the train pass with nobody looking out, the fireman shovelling, and the driver apparently asleep, so telephoned Horsham. The fireman, seeing the signals at danger, stopped the train at the station, where an inspector was waiting with another driver.

The fireman explained what had happened, the driver was carried off the engine, and the train resumed its journey in the charge of the Horsham driver. It did not take a doctor long to find out that the driver, far from being drunk, was very ill, and he was taken to the local hospital. Anyway, to cut a long story short, when the facts were reported to Bob Billinton, he had the driver and fireman on the carpet; but being in a good mood that day, he just gave them a sort of fatherly lecture, telling the driver that the company was not a slave-driver, and that he should not have reported for work before he was thoroughly fit. He told the fireman that while appreciating his loyalty to his mate and his endeavour to prevent any traffic delay, he should also remember that the first rule of every railwayman should be 'play for safety', and his duty was to have stopped at the first station or signal box and asked for assistance. That 'closed the case'.

Old Bob was sound at heart, and when not troubled by his complaint, had a sense of humour. One morning at London Bridge he saw the driver of a main line train, just arrived from the South Coast, sitting on the seatbox having a rest and a smoke while waiting for the station pilot to pull out the empty coaches. The driver was smoking a clay pipe, and old Bob told him that it was a reflection on the company to do that in full view of passengers. If he couldn't afford a respectable cigar, he should go down and have his smoke by the side of the engine away from the platform, where he would not be seen!

Talking of passengers, the LB&SCR was pre-eminently a passenger-carrying line, and we certainly carried all sorts, shapes, sizes and conditions. One class we absolutely detested were the snobs. A character in one of Charles Dickens's books, who had a very exaggerated idea of his own importance, was highly indignant because the fireman of the train he was about to travel on, dared to address him. 'An ignorant churl in a dirty canvas suit' was his description of the fireman; but Toodles (as Dickens called him) knew his job, as the train arrived on time. Such people exist in real life. I remember once we were standing at London Bridge, when a few minutes before departure time a fat pompous-looking man came up to the engine, with two small boys. He did not speak to us, but just pointed to ourselves and two or three things on the footplate, then leaving the boys standing by the cab, he stood back from the engine, with the most conceited look of smug superiority on his face that I ever remember seeing. It took all the will-power that I possessed to refrain from planting a nice wet oily 'socker' right in the middle of it, and causing him to alter his expression; what my mate remarked would set this paper alight if I put it down.

One November evening we lost five minutes on a run up from Eastbourne with a heavy load through dense patches of fog, over rails that were as slippery as a frozen pond. We thought we had done pretty well, but as a party of four 'aristocrats' passed the engine, one of them remarked in a voice intended for us to hear, 'The drivers on this line don't trouble about timekeeping, their ideas want waking up!' I said to my mate, 'They ought to be thankful they got here at all, after the trip we've had'. Some folk are never satisfied!

Very different was the comment of a cockney youth at Brighton. The train was the relief Restall excursion. Restall's of Cheapside hired trains for cheap trips on early-closing days and as the fare to Brighton and back was only half-a-crown they were well patronised, as you can imagine. The advertised time for departure from London Bridge was 12.55 pm calling at New Cross 1.0 and East Croydon 1.15 pm. There were usually enough passengers for two trains, and sometimes three; and as most of the trippers got to London Bridge in good time to get a seat, reliefs were run ahead of the advertised train, being despatched by the platform inspector as soon as they were full, and running non-stop to Preston Park where tickets were collected. Brighton was then an 'open' station.

We had No. 348 *Lullington*, one of the single-wheelers, and a 'workmen' set of 14 four-wheel open thirds with no partitions between the compartments, about the lightest rolling stock that the LB&SCR possessed. We got the 'right away' at 12.45; 'Lullie' was in good fettle, and with an absolutely clear road and a bit of good Welsh coal in the tender she knocked off the 48½ miles to Preston Park in 50 minutes easily. Tickets were duly collected, and we pulled along to the terminus. As the before-mentioned cockney lad passed the engine, he paused and said with a cheery smile 'We 'eard as 'ow these 'ere cheap trips was slow, but corblimey, matey, yer didn't 'arf 'op it!' The trippers did not mind how fast we went, or how much they were shaken up, as long as they arrived all right; but the guard, on this particular occasion, asked for a little more leisurely return trip. He said that the way the light four-wheel brake van wagged its tail at over 70 mph gave him a queer feeling inside!

Billinton class 'C2' 'Vulcan' 0-6-0 No. 555 on Newhaven Shed receives a final oil up prior to departing with one of the many well loaded goods workings out of the docks.
Author's Collection

Stroudley 'G' class 'Single' No. 337 *Yarmouth* built in 1881, receives last minute attention before departure from Eastbourne in 1903.

M.P. Bennett/Bluebell Archives

Chapter Eleven

The 'Linger and Die' Route

Mention of cheap excursions brings to mind another rather uncommon practice connected with them. As I remarked once before, the LB&SCR was among the pioneers of electric lighting in the coaches and a number of the 10-coach suburban sets of four-wheelers had electric lamps. Current was supplied from accumulators in one of the guards' vans, and they were kept charged by a big dynamo, also in the vans, and driven from a pulley on one of the axles by a hefty belt coming up through a hole in the floor. It was not until the advent of the seven-coach bogie sets, around the turn of the century, that the system of a separate small dynamo and battery for each coach, all mounted under the floor, came into use. Before that, all separate coaches not made up into sets were provided with oil-gas lighting. The gas was stored in cylinders under the floor, and a pressure gauge was fitted below the footboards, so that carriage examiners could see at a glance how much gas was in each cylinder. Charging was usually done at the carriage sidings.

In the earlier days of oil lighting, when a row of little chimneys decorated the roof of each coach, lamps were lit only during the hours of darkness. Passengers between London and Brighton had a blackout ride through the three long tunnels - Merstham, Balcombe, and Clayton. However, after a murder was committed in Balcombe tunnel in an unlighted compartment, the newspapers kicked up such a shindy that something had to be done about it. An experiment with lights in the tunnels themselves proving a washout, the order went forth that all trains on the route through long tunnels must always have lights in the coaches. Short tunnel routes were not affected.

When so many passengers turned up for excursion trips that extra relief trains had to be run, there was always a desperate scramble for coaches, and anything available in the sidings was hastily pressed into service. The result was that some of the relief London Bridge-Brighton excursion trains around the turn of the century were made up of from 10 to 15 'spares', four- and six-wheeled stock with oil-gas lighting. As soon as they were backed into the platform road, a 'wheeltapper' (carriage examiner) would go along and look at the gas gauges under the footboards. If there was plenty of gas, sufficient for the return trip via the direct route through the long tunnels, the train went that way. If not, the train went via the 'Linger and Die' route (Dorking, Horsham, Henfield and Shoreham) on which there were only short tunnels. The consequence was, that if we happened to be commandeered for a relief excursion trip, we did not know which way we were going, until informed by the platform inspector a few minutes before starting!

Many enginemen preferred the 'Linger and Die' route; though it was considerably longer, it was a far more pleasant run, easier graded, and much less congested than the direct line. In fact, I do not recollect ever being stopped by signal when going that way, whereas there were usually several signal stops on the main line between London Bridge and Redhill. South Eastern trains bound for the Redhill-Tonbridge and Redhill-Guildford lines seemed to take an unholy delight in getting in the way of the LB&SCR trains! They weren't so bad on the Oxted line between East Croydon and Crowhurst Junction North, where they disappeared down the spur toward Edenbridge.

Mention of the 'Linger and Die' recalls an amazing feat performed by one of the Stroudley single-wheelers. Those good folk who 'prove' by slide-rule calculation that the tractive effort of a railway locomotive is limited by the weight on the driving-wheels would swear by all the gods that it was impossible, yet it was actually done. On 23rd December, 1899, the up boat train from Newhaven Harbour was stopped by signal at Wivelsfield in a dense fog, and the 5 pm from Brighton ran into the back of it, for the driver was unable to see the signals. The main line was completely blocked and traffic disorganised.

Later that night, in an endeavour to sort things out, the coaches for three complete trains were combined into one, and despatched to London via the 'Linger and Die' route. The only available engine was a single-wheeler No. 337 *Yarmouth*. Now if you can imagine a load of 27 coaches, made up of four-wheelers, six-wheelers and bogies, totting up to nearly 300 tons, and a small engine with less than 14 tons on its solitary pair of driving wheels, cylinders 17 in. x 24 in. and 150 lb. of 'wet' steam, at the head of such a train, you may get some idea of the task facing the driver and fireman. Well, they just went ahead and achieved the 'impossible'. When *Yarmouth* pulled into London Bridge with her outsize in loads, the smokebox door was red hot up to the crossbar. When the driver was asked how he managed to get up Ockley Bank, he just gave a weary sort of grin and said 'I'm ————— if I know - but we're here!' Ockley Bank, between Ockley and Warnham, is roughly three miles long, the middle mile rising toward London at 1 in 90, and the other two at 1 in 100. 'Twas ever thus! Before the Rainhill trials back in 1829, two eminent engineers of the day, Messrs Rastrick and Walker, predicted that the adhesion of the one pair of driving wheels on the *Rocket* was barely sufficient to take her own weight up Rainhill Bank, and she would never be able to haul a load. George Stephenson promptly put the tin hat on that assertion by taking up a coach with a load of passengers at 20 mph. Back in 1921 I was accused of being a shocking liar when I said that I had built a 2½ in. gauge coal-fired steam locomotive that could pull my weight easily. The laugh was on my side when I took the little engine to the Caxton Hall, Westminster, and she confounded all the 'experts' by doing it, right before their eyes. History has a knack of repeating itself!

Four days before the accident recorded above there was a similar pitch-in, also in dense fog. Teddy Herriott, driving No. 388 *Emsworth* (one of the Billinton bogie tanks) on the 8.10 am London Bridge to Oxted, ran into the back of the 8.7 am South London line train, which was stopped by signal at South Bermondsey. The lines out of London Bridge run on a brick viaduct, and the signal that Teddy missed in the fog was on the parapet wall, on his right, with two up lines between him and the signal. I was in New Cross yard when the damaged engine was pulled in, with the chimney knocked right off, and the front badly battered. Then, when news of the other wreck came through four days later, and a driver commented that in foggy weather we needed signals in the cab, I had an idea.

All the Brighton trains were fitted with the Stroudley-Rusbridge electric passenger alarm. By pulling a knob in the wall of the compartment, in case of emergency, passengers could ring the alarm bells on the engine and in the guards' vans. The bell on the engine received its supply of 'juice' from a dry battery carried in the tool box. It occurred to me that if some gadget could be fixed up so that the bell could be given just a tinkle when approaching a distant signal, any chance of overlooking one in fog or snow would be greatly minimised. One thought led to another, to cut a long story short, I eventually schemed out a device that indicated whether the signal was 'on' or 'off'. It was quite simple. A trip close to the rail, something like a short point-locking bar, was connected to the signal wire, so that it operated automatically. A contact on the engine was arranged so that when the trip was down, and the signal 'off', the alarm bell gave just one short ring. If the trip was up, and the signal 'on', a red light was shown in the cab. This was a miniature signal lamp with a red glass, and a torch bulb inside, lit by current from the bell battery.

Here, thought I, is the complete answer to safe working in fog; and in the innocence of my heart, I thought that it would be welcomed by the company and fitted to all the engines and signals. Accidents due to missing signals in fog would be avoided completely, a big load would be taken off the minds of engine crews, and the company would have no more compensation to pay out. Alas for my hopes! It was turned down flat, on account of the expense of installing it, the excuse being that the very small number of accidents did not justify the outlay. The fact that the very small number of accidents was entirely due to the vigilance of the enginemen was entirely overlooked! I was advised that as I had no money to patent the device, I had better keep the details to myself. Thoroughly downhearted and disappointed, I did; but you can imagine my feelings when a similar arrangement was brought out many years later in America, and cab signalling became common on USA railroads. Their method of operation was different from mine, and the cab lamp showed green, yellow or red lights, like the trackside signals; but the fundamental idea was the same. Maybe if I had met some American railroad magnate in 1900 and offered him the device, my life would have taken a different course - such is fate!

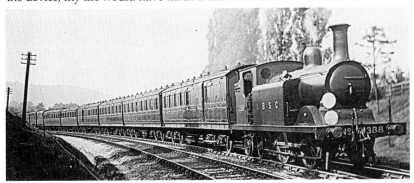

No. 388 having lost its name and in Marsh livery, brings a heavily loaded train up the 1 in 90 gradient south of Dorking station. The presence of horse boxes at the rear makes one surmise whether this might be one of the horse and hound 'Hunt Specials' the LB&SCR ran in pre-1914 days.   *H. Gordon Tidey/Lens of Sutton*

Robert Billinton's 'Bogie Tanks' were amongst the LB&SCR's most handsome engines. No. 382 *Farlington* (*above*) stands at New Cross Shed with driver William Armes (*right*) on the track beside the bunker with his fireman, while (*below*) No. 388 *Emsworth*, (*see page 66*) also from the same depot, is out on a turn of duty at Hove. *(Both) Lens of Sutton*

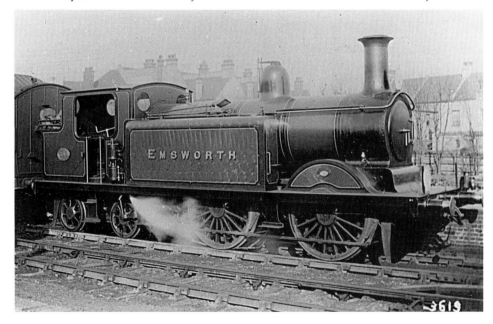

Chapter Twelve

From Wimbledon to Woppleton
and Back From Singleton

One evening we were working a suburban trip, the 8.13 pm Wimbledon 'roundabout'. This was an easy jog-trot calling at all stations between London Bridge and Wimbledon, and was known as a 'roundabout' because it went via Haydon's Road on the outward journey, did not reverse at Wimbledon, but carried right on and returned via the Merton Abbey loop line to Tooting Junction, where it rejoined the outward route. The engine was one of the Billinton bogie tanks, No. 382 *Farlington* to the best of my recollection, and she was running bunker first. Some drivers preferred to run chimney first wherever possible, as they found it more convenient to operate regulator, brake valve and reverser when looking the way they were going. Others preferred to run bunker first, as there was no smoke or steam blowing around the cab windows, and they reckoned that tank engines ran steadier with an uncoupled wheel leading.

There was, however, one drawback to running bunker first. When the fireman wanted to pop in a few black diamonds while running, and pulled up the sliding coal gate, the draught down the bunker blew a lot of coal dust into the cab, which was not very pleasant, to say the least, so most of them fired at stations or when running slowly. Some drivers did not care a bean which way they ran, but tell it not in Gath - two or three of my acquaintances were too darn lazy to bother about going on the turntable and pushing their engines around by hand. There were no power-operated turntables in those days, and it needed a little skill to balance the engine in the middle, so that pushing was comparatively easy.

Well we duly arrived at Wimbledon, set down the remaining passengers, picked up a few for the return trip, and departed at 8.53 as per timetable. There is a very sharp curve between Wimbledon and Merton Park, and the engine did not seem to like this at all on that particular evening, although she had been around it many times before without complaint. She started to grind and quiver, then suddenly there was a crack, and the trailing end which was leading swung over a little to the left; then she ran quite freely. I guessed what had happened; the bogie side-control spring had broken, and so it proved. This left the bogie free to oscillate, but on the curves there was no appreciable difference in the running. We called at Merton Park, Merton Abbey, Tooting, and Streatham and, as these stations are fairly close together and there is not much straight line between them, we did not make any speed worth writing home about, and the journey was just normal.

Between Streatham and Tulse Hill the line is a bit straighter, but it rises towards London, so we did not go very fast on that bit either; but it was after leaving Tulse Hill that the fun started. From there to Peckham Rye there is a falling gradient and, as the engine picked up speed through Knight's Hill Tunnel and came out on to the viaduct, the uncontrolled bogie started 'hunting', and the cab swayed from side to side. There was no danger, but it was decidedly uncomfortable. My mate was one of those delightful characters who can extract a spot of humour out of almost anything, and he didn't fail on this

Class 'B4' 4-4-0 No. 60 *Kimberley* waits at Singleton in 1909 with the return Royal Train bringing King Edward VII back from a day out - and a wet one at that! - at Goodwood Races.

Lens of Sutton

'G' class 2-2-2 No. 350 *Southbourne*, in the cleanest Brighton condition, rests outside Littlehampton Shed in 1901 after working a special from London.

O.J. Morris Collection/Bluebell Archives

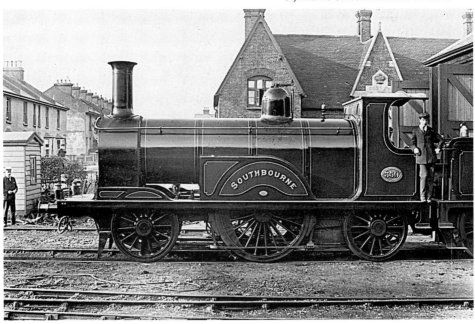

occasion, for he started singing, in time to the movement of the cab,

From Wimbledon to Woppleton is fourteen miles
From Woppleton to Wimbledon is fourteen miles
From Wimbledon to Woppleton, from Woppleton to Wimbledon,
From Wimbledon to Woppleton is fourteen miles

He kept it up all the way to the junction at Peckham Rye, where we had to cross from main to local, as there were no platforms to the main line at Old Kent Road and South Bermondsey. The engine gave a violent lurch as she took the facing points of the crossover, causing him to sit down with a mighty bump on the coal-dust-covered footboard, which promptly put an end to his vocal efforts, the 'Amen' being in 'railroad Esperanto'!

Incidentally, I knew another singing engineman who was a driver on the London Chatham and Dover suburban lines. Between Sydenham Hill and Penge, on their main line, is a long tunnel going under the Crystal Palace grounds. Travellers on the LB&SCR can see the southern portal where the LC&DR passes underneath, between Sydenham and Penge. Whenever this driver worked a Holborn or Victoria to Bickley local train, which goes through the tunnel, he would start singing 'Annie Laurie' as the train pulled out of Sydenham Hill Station and entered the tunnel. This always puzzled the firemen, until he explained, and the explanation was not only simple, but ingenious.

Penge LC&DR station was close to the tunnel exit and the down distant signal was some distance inside the tunnel, difficult to spot when the tunnel was full of steam and smoke, as it usually was. The driver said that if he started the ballad as he entered the tunnel, by the time he got to 'Lay me doon and dee' it was time to look out for Penge down distant, and so far he had never missed it!

Writing about tunnels reminds me of those on the single line between Chichester and Midhurst, long since closed - more's the pity! For some reason they were always damp, and the rails through them were in consequence rather slippery. Being single line, the bores were not very big either, and the trains nearly filled them when passing through, leaving little clearance for steam and smoke to get away. One of the stations, Singleton, was close to Goodwood Racecourse, and as there were very few motor cars in those days of long ago (the few that existed were of the Harry Tate variety) the racing fraternity travelling from London were catered for by the LB&SCR by through trains to Singleton. Most of the specials were composed of any old stock that was available like the cheap excursions I have previously mentioned.

One evening we left Singleton for London Bridge with a race special. The load was a 10-coach set of four-wheeled suburban stock plus three or four 'spares'. There was no 'class distinction' on the race specials; one fare only was charged, and the fraternity rode in any compartment. No ticket collector would ever have risked his anatomy by trying to collect excess fare from a racegoer travelling in a first-class compartment with a third-class ticket! The engine was a single-wheeler, No. 350 *Southbourne* if memory serves me right, and she was due for shopping. Anything that could run had to be pressed into service for race specials, but the Brighton drivers being trained (no pun intended!) in the hard school of experience, could get along with almost anything on wheels. She slipped pretty badly getting away from the station, as the sanders were not working properly and the sand was rather damp. It was only gravity fed; what we called a 'drop sander'. Only the 'Gladstones' among the Stroudley engines had steam sanders, operated via a short pipe from the steam-chest underneath the cylinders. The Billinton engines had steam sanders, but as the steam had to run through long pipes from the valve on the backhead in the cab, right down to the sand ejectors, it was water by the time it arrived, and the sanders were not very effective. When it was suggested to old Bob that compressed air from the air brake reservoirs would be far better, he nearly had a fit.

Anyway, we got going, but there were two tunnels between Singleton and Cocking; we got through the first one fairly well, but the rise through Cocking Tunnel plus the damp rails, started another attack of slipping and, as the sanders had now given up the ghost altogether, we were in a proper mess. On top of that, the coal was a mixture of Yorkshire hard, and what we called 'dum-dum', both very smoky, and what was put on before leaving Singleton had not burnt clear. The heavy blast caused by the slipping caused the steam and smoke to beat down into the cab like a dense fog, and not only nearly gassed the pair of us, but drifted back along the narrow space between tunnel and coaches, and caused a frantic slamming of carriage windows. However, we eventually got clear, and as luck would have it, the evening was dry, and the rails in the open air also being dry, the lack of sand caused no further delay. The old engine put her back into it, and once she got going, she kept it up. We had lost a few minutes owing to the slipping antics, but now had a clear road; and not having to stop at Horsham, we were able to 'rush' Ockley Bank and got over it in fine style. The rest was plain sailing, or rather plain steaming, and we landed at London Bridge on time. We expected some hearty votes of thanks from the lads of the villages for nearly poisoning them in Cocking Tunnel, especially from those who had backed all the losers, but they weren't too bad, mostly good-humoured. Race specials made a pleasant break from the usual routine working, so incidentally did school treats.

Stroudley 'D' tanks were to be seen in profusion all over the Brighton system. No. 240 *Ditchling*, a New Cross engine, makes a stop at Forest Hill with a London Bridge-bound local, the track ballasted over the sleepers indicating a date prior to 1900. *Lens of Sutton*

Chapter Thirteen

A Dirty Trick and Some Strange Trips

Writing this at the August Bank Holiday week-end reminds me of another August Bank Holiday, when one of the Stroudley tanks - I believe it was No. 240 *Ditchling* - played a literally dirty trick on some holidaymakers at Boxhill station. We were working an evening train from Dorking to London Bridge. The engine was steaming and pulling all right, but the boiler was badly in need of a wash-out. In fact she would have got it, but at holiday times everything that could pull a train had to be pressed into service. Now when a boiler is dirty, that is, choked up with 'fur' and scale, like you see in a well-used domestic kettle, the water becomes frothy and bubbles up after the style of mum's wash-boiler. If the regulator is opened suddenly, water will go over into the cylinders with the steam, and be blown from the chimney along with the exhaust; the enginemen call it 'priming'.

We were late leaving Dorking owing to platform delay - you probably know what it is like on Bank Holidays! - and made a frantic spurt to Boxhill. The old girl was blowing off fairly hard as we pulled alongside the platform, crowded with returning trippers, Boxhill being a favourite place for an afternoon out. If the Stroudley air brake valve is turned to 'stop' position and left there, the train pulls up with a violent jerk and 'back-kick', so the proper procedure is to make a 'two-application stop'; first, what we called a service application to check from running speed, then release, then another gentle application which ensured a perfectly smooth stop provided that the triple-valves (the automatic brake valves under the coaches, controlling the admission and release of air to the brake cylinders) were working properly. On the train we were pulling they were a bit sluggish; this, combined with our quicker-than-usual run in, resulted in a jerky stop. The blower was on as well, because if the blower is not put on before the regulator is shut the draught down the chimney will blow flames out of the firehole door, and the driver and fireman might receive serious burns.

Most of the women and girls on the crowded platform were wearing the fashionable summer attire of the period; white or light-coloured silk or cotton blouses, high-necked, with balloon or leg-of-mutton sleeves, plenty of lace and embroidery, full skirts down to their feet (we called them platform-sweepers) and big floppy hats or sun-bonnets. As the engine stopped, the jerk made the water in the boiler surge violently, and the boiler being pretty well full, the result was a sudden upsurge of dirty water along with the steam from the safety valves. The surge also caused another rush to go over with the steam operating the blower, and this roared out of the chimney, taking plenty of soot with it. There was a slight breeze blowing, and in a matter of seconds, the whole blessed lot came down all over the trippers. Talk about a mess! There was some screaming, lamentations and what-have-you, but they all got in the train, and had dried out by the time we reached London Bridge. There were a few uncomplimentary remarks as soiled femininity passed the engine, and, as modern detergents were unknown in those days, I should imagine that a few

'Terrier' No. 49 *Bishopsgate* stands at New Cross with Aspinall's Enamel Work, a background landmark in so many New Cross Shed photographs, visible in front of No. 49's smokebox. It was among the earlier members of the class to be sold out of service in 1902 to Messrs Pauling & Co., contractors of the Northolt to High Wycombe extension of the Great Western and Great Central Railways.   *Lens of Sutton*

'Terrier' No. 49 *Bishopsgate* in the service of Messrs Pauling & Co This shot was taken early one Sunday morning in 1903 at Northolt. Above the name on the side tank is the legend 'P & Co Ltd No 79', while the gilt number 649 still appeared on the bunker. Behind stands one of Pauling's saddle tanks, No. 56 *Northolt*, complete with separate brass number and name plates on the tank sides.   *Lens of Sutton*

extra cakes of 'Sunlight' were called for the next washday to get the stains out!

There was a guard working on the East London line about the turn of the century, who was nicknamed the 'drum-major' from the peculiar habit of waving his flag like the soldier who walks ahead of a regimental band waving a gadget, the name of which I don't know. One day this party was working on a train from Peckham Rye to Shoreditch, and when giving the driver the 'right-away' with the usual drum-major flag-flourish, the handle somehow slipped through his fingers. The flag sailed right over the roof of the van and fell in front of a District train just running into the station on the opposite road. Naturally the flag was not of much further use after the District engine had run over it, but the drum-major did not know that, as he had to hop into his van pretty quick, the Brighton train being already on the move.

The main line trains carried a couple of spare flags and a few fog-signals as per the rule book, for the protection of trains in case of breakdown, but there were no spare flags on the East London local sets. However, that did not daunt our hero. At the first available bookstall he got a periodical with a green cover (*Tit-Bits* as far as I recollect) tore off the paper cover, tied it to a piece of stick, and carried on with that for the rest of his spell of duty. It was a pity that the publishers didn't know - it would have been a fine advertisement for them, and probably have brought the guard a reward for his ingenuity.

Mention of the District Railway calls to mind the only occasion, to the best of my knowledge and belief, that a Brighton engine took the left-hand fork at Whitechapel Jn and went exploring the District territory. In those far-off days, the railways always helped one another in time of trouble and emergency, even though they might be rivals; but it was always done 'officially' to a predetermined plan. In the instance I am about to relate it was a spot of quick thinking, plus prompt action on the part of the railwaymen concerned, that saved inconvenience to a number of passengers and expense to the District Company.

At that period, the five-day week was just a dream; most working folk received their weekly wages after knocking off early on Saturday afternoon, and most of the weekly shopping was done on Saturday night. Pubs and shops stayed open till midnight. Consequently, there were plenty of passengers travelling on the last trains. Both District and Metropolitan trains ran to New Cross via the East London line, the former using the LB&SCR station and the latter the South Eastern. On the Saturday night in question, the engine of the last District train failed with a burst tube, a most unusual thing to happen to one of those old reliable hard-working locomotives. There was a tidy crowd in the train waiting to go, and it looked as if the whole lot would be stranded, when the driver of a 'Terrier' who had finished his turn, and was waiting to cross over to the sheds (memory grows dim, but I believe it was Fred Parker, driving No. 49 *Bishopsgate*) offered to run the District train, with the driver of the disabled engine as pilotman, if it could be arranged on the quick. This was possible, because the District trains had the same brakes as the Brighton trains (Westinghouse air brake), so the Brighton engine could operate it. Had it been a Metropolitan train, this would have been impossible, as they had vacuum brakes, and no 'Terrier' had vacuum equipment, though a few of the main line

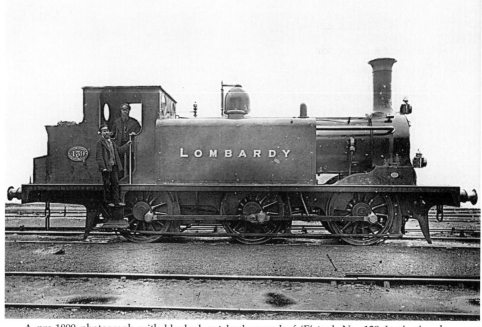

A pre-1899 photograph with blanked out background of 'E' tank No. 139 *Lombardy* whose collision with *Crowhurst* is described in the adjoining pages. The location is adjudged to be Battersea, though *Lombardy* was a New Cross engine.   *John Minnis Collection*

No. 224 *Crowhurst* of Battersea Shed pauses between the platforms at Victoria. Note the temporary roof and beams while the terminus was being rebuilt, work completed in 1908, also the decrepit paintwork on No. 224 underlining how hard an existence life on the London suburban services was for both locomotive and crew.   *Lens of Sutton*

engines had it for working through trains from the LNWR and other 'vacuum lines'.

There was a hurried consultation between the night locomotive foreman and the relief station master, and it was decided to act. The District engine was pulled off the train, the 'Terrier' backed on and duly departed on her unexpected trip into the unknown. The load of nine District four-wheelers did not worry her and the way she trotted them up the grade from the Thames Tunnel to Wapping station was an eye-opener to the District driver. Meantime the telephone had been busy, and arrangements had been made for a District engine to meet her at Earl's Court, and take the train on to its destination. She made the run in fine style, though she left more steam in the tunnels than a District engine which had full condensing gear, and returned light, with the District driver still acting as pilotman.

While she was away, the night locomotive foreman thought that he might as well finish the job, so he got the yard pilot engine to go across to the East London sidings and bring the casualty into the yard. The night-shift boilermaker and his mate had no difficulty in plugging the ends of the burst tube with a couple of taper plugs and a stay rod. She was lit up again, and the District driver was able to take her home under her own steam, thus avoiding the trouble and expense of her owners sending a rescue team, or towing her home.

The incident was known to very few folk outside the people who actually took part in it, and it was never placed on record. It was, of course, reported, but how the companies settled the business side of the operation we neither knew nor cared. All we did know was that the District Company paid tribute to the resourcefulness and initiative of the LB&SCR men and what was more to the point, backed it up with a cash present. Such an incident could never happen nowadays - too much red tape attached to it!

One engine made an unexpected trip all on her own in 1899, that was No. 139 *Lombardy*, one of the Stroudley 'E' class 0-6-0 goods tanks. She had left the yard, and was crossing over to the down local line, when due to a signalman's error, she was run into by a down local train headed by No. 224 *Crowhurst*. The driver of the latter, which was running bunker first, saw the goods engine in his way, and did his best to stop clear, which he very nearly did; but his full bunker was bumped into *Lombardy* with a tidy wallop. The driver and fireman of the latter, seeing that a collision was inevitable, jumped off, but in his haste, the driver left the regulator partly open. The lever being in forward gear, off went *Lombardy* all on her own, heading for the Sunny South.

News of the runaway was hastily telephoned down the line, and a path was cleared for her, but she did not get very far. She managed to get through Norwood Junction and East Croydon without mishap, but the signalman at South Croydon Junction box stopped her gallop. He held the points at the junction leading to Selsdon Road at 'half-cock', instead of throwing them right over, and when the engine hit them, she jumped the road and stopped. Little damage was done, and nobody was hurt, which was fortunate, as the consequences might have been serious if she had overtaken a passenger train.

'D' tank No. 9 *Anerley* belonged to the second batch of 1874. The first 12 were all based at New Cross Shed where this picture was taken in 1901. The tool box at the rear of the bunker provides a comfortable seat for the shedhand. *M.P. Bennett/Bluebell Archives*

Class 'E4' 0-6-2T No. 565 *Littleton* commenced working from Battersea Shed as an oil burner on 1st May, 1902, using the Bell & Holden's injector system. The oil tank can be seen on the bunker. Following trials in the London area it was allocated to Horsham Shed. Here it is seen on Brighton Shed, posed in a setting between water columns which also includes an artistic shed lamp and bracket. Its superb state of turnout betokens the fact that it was still a comparatively new engine, for this fine portrait must have been taken before August 1903 when this locomotive was converted to coal burning. *M.P. Bennett/Bluebell Archives*

Chapter Fourteen

A Dangerous Dare and Billinton's 'Scotchmen' are Shown Up

A few evenings ago the radio announcer reading the news bulletin gave an account of some children at Hatfield playing the insane antic of 'last across the line' in front of express trains on the old Great Northern main line, and warned parents to take every precaution to prevent the kids flirting with death. This reminded me of an incident that occurred at Tooting Common one Saturday afternoon in the spring of 1903. We were working the 2.58 pm London Bridge to Norwood Junction and Victoria, an all-stations jog-trot which landed at Victoria just after four. I believe the engine was No. 9 *Anerley* but would not swear to it after all these years.

At that time the road across Tooting Common was little more than a glorified country lane, and it crossed the railway just south of Balham Intermediate signal box by a narrow arched bridge, with a long ramp at each end, the road being very little higher than the railway. It was a long bridge, as it spanned four lines, and although there were very few motor vehicles in those days, there were plenty of wide horse-drawn outfits, such as brewers' drays and so on. It would have been very close quarters if a pedestrian had met one of these in the middle of the bridge, so an iron footbridge had been put up a few yards on the south side. This was of the usual girder type, with a stairway at each end; and as it was narrow, smoke deflector boards were fixed to the underside, directly above each line. There was not much clearance between the bottom of the bridge and the engine chimney-tops. If two women wearing the platform-sweeper skirts of those days had been passing each other just as a heavily-loaded goods engine had been passing underneath, something would certainly have happened if the smoke boards had not been there!

We were a couple of minutes or so behind time, and were taking advantage of the fairly long stretch between Streatham Common and Balham to get a move on, and pick it up a little. As we came in sight of the footbridge, my heart jumped up in my throat. Sitting astride the smoke board above the line we were on, was a small boy, and on the bridge were several others watching him. There was no earthly chance of stopping before reaching the bridge; the only thing to do was shut off steam, give a good long blast on the whistle, and trust to providence that he would not fall as the train passed under. The boy was holding something, but he never attempted to throw. As we passed under the smoke board, there was a crash against the front of the cab, and I saw what was apparently a piece of a broken brick lying on the side tank. When we stopped at Balham, I told the station master, and he said he would telephone the signal box, also send a porter down on the next train, and get the driver to let him off near the bridge, by the down Intermediate starting signals.

This was done, and we heard afterwards that the porter got on to the footbridge before being spotted by the kids. Those on the bridge lost no time in scooting off, but he caught the one who had been on the smoke board. This imp of mischief said that the other boys had dared him to drop the piece of brick

Robert Billinton's 'B2' class 4-4-0 No. 206 *Smeaton*, which made its name with the inaugural under-the-hour run with the 'Pullman Limited' to Brighton in the autumn of 1898, is seen (*above*) passing Balham Intermediate box on its way through Tooting with a coastbound express containing a clerestory Pullman car at the turn of the century, and (*below*) shunting stock in the centre road at Eastbourne station.   *Dr T.S. Budden and M.P. Bennett/Bluebell Archives*

down one of the engine chimneys. Whether the company took him to the juvenile court for attempted damage, I don't know; but in my humble opinion, the finest cure for that sort of thing - and for the 'last-across-the-line' merchants, is a darn good tanning. If the piece of brick had smashed through the cab window and caught my mate or myself in the face, it would have been a hospital job, if nothing worse, probably resulting in loss of eyesight.

Incidentally, by a million-to-one chance, something actually did go down the chimney of a moving engine. One of the Battersea firemen, when raking the ashes out of the smokebox of No. 351 *Chailey*, found the charred remains of a cricket ball. The engine had crossed both Tooting Common and Wandsworth Common several times during the day; the ball must have been skied by a super-energetic batsman, and gone down the chimney when the engine was coasting with steam off. Several cricket pitches were close to the line, within easy slogging distance. The score book should have read 'Jones, c. *Chailey*, b. Smith'!

Toward the end of the last century the station at Heathfield was lit by natural gas, apparently coming up from an underground accumulation of oil. It was decided to try and find the source, and ascertain whether there was enough oil to use as fuel for the engines. Jimmy Holden, the locomotive superintendent of the Great Eastern Railway was then successfully using the residue from the oil-gas plant at Stratford, hitherto wasted, on quite a number of the GER locomotives. The oil was duly found, and one of the radial tanks, No. 565 *Littleton*, was fitted up with oil-burning apparatus. She did most of her trial running on the South London line, London Bridge to Victoria via Denmark Hill, Brixton, and Clapham. She steamed all right, and they reckoned it was cheaper than coal; but oh, boy! did she niff? The perfume she gave off with the oil burners in full blast was very similar to frying kippers.

It was a standing joke among the staff at London Bridge, that you could smell her starting away from Victoria, and tell where she was on the journey, by the density of the atmosphere!

Anyway, the experiment was apparently satisfactory to Bob Billinton and the Directors of the company for several more engines were fitted with oil burners, including a 'Gladstone', one of the 5 ft 6 in. radial tanks, and No. 206 *Smeaton*, a Billinton 4-4-0. Just as everything in the garden was apparently going to be lovely, bar the perfume, the oil well dried up. Heathfield lost its free gas supply, and the engines lost their oil burners. I might mention here, that this was not the first time oil firing had been tried on the LB&SCR. Long before, one of the Stroudley tanks, No. 27 *Uckfield*, had a Tarbutt oil burner fitted, but it was not in the same street with the Holden burner. They had not the experience, and, as the results were inferior to coal burning, the Tarbutt oil apparatus was scrapped.

I recollect the song and dance that took place when the first of old Bob's big 4-4-0s ('B4' class) came out in 1899, round about Christmas time, No. 52 *Siemens*. Many wondered why on earth she had that 'moniker' bestowed on her, but as the previous one (the enlarged grasshopper) was named *Bessemer* another name connected with steel was only logical. Her driver was a grumpy old kite named Harry Aylwin, and the first day she came into New Cross Shed after working a train up from Brighton, naturally some of the cleaner boys gathered around her to take a look. Old Harry ordered them all away, as if she were a top priority

Two of Robert Billinton's 'Scotchmen' photographed on the New Cross turntable in 1901. No. 56 *Roberts*, named after the Boer War general, was a New Cross engine and a true 'Scot' built by Sharp, Stewart & Co. and delivered in July 1901 so was as good as new when this picture was taken. No. 52 *Siemens* (*middle*) was the first of the class to appear in 1899, built at Brighton and allocated to that shed. In September 1908 it was renamed *Sussex* and is seen below peeping out of the New Shed at New Cross.   (*All*) *M.P. Bennett/Bluebell Archives*

'D' tank No. 27 *Uckfield* inside the back of Brighton Works in April 1907, undergoing a major repair, and losing its name to emerge in the new Marsh umber livery. Engines of this class going through Works at this period were fitted with a new steel boiler to replace the Stroudley one which had been in use in some cases since 1873 and often for more than 700,000 miles. Back in 1886 No. 27 had been the subject of a shortlived experiment, being fitted with Tarbutt's oil burning equipment. *M.P. Bennett/Bluebell Archives*

'B4' 4-4-0 class No. 49 *Queensland*, and a true 'Scotchman' at that, stands immaculate in all its glory. The pose and setting and position of the headlamps suggest an official photograph, possibly on the east side of the running lines opposite Lovers Walk, and may well have been taken when the locomotive entered service in August 1901. *M.P. Bennett/Bluebell Archives*

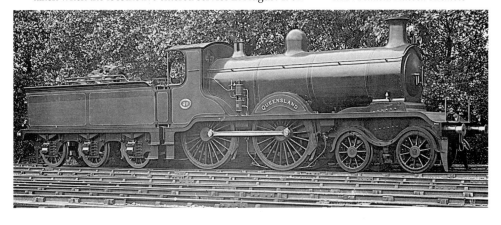

The 'G' class 'Singles', built between 1874 and 1882, were described when new as 'Mr Stroudley's 2-2-2 express locomotives'. They were still on main line duties until well into the first decade of the new century, but promptly retired when Earle Marsh took office. *Above*, No. 331 *Fairlight* heads a special to Hastings approaching Wivelsfield Junction while, *below*, No. 333 *Ventnor*, with a dozen carriages behind, leaves the south portal of Clayton Tunnel with another special to the coast.   *M.P. Bennett/Bluebell Archives*

secret. The semi-technical press went into ecstasy, and Clement Stretton and other writers of the period reckoned the class would revolutionise the LB&SCR express services. Well, it just didn't. The 'Gladstones' could easily have anticipated 'Annie-get-your-gun' by singing - with perfect truth - 'Anything that you can do, I can do better'.

The firm of Sharp, Stewart built 25 of the 'B4s', and they were delivered via the East London line, all the superfluous knobs and excrescences likely to foul the East London tunnels and platforms being temporarily removed. I was over in the East London sidings on the morning that No. 49 *Queensland* came through, in the summer of 1901, and had a friendly chat with the dour old Scot who accompanied them to that point, from where the LB&SCR took them over. I asked him what his personal opinions were, about these particular engines, compared with other jobs he had delivered to other railways. He said that if the LB&SCR had paid a little more than the price of tomatoes for the engines, they would have done better, and he reckoned that the tubes would all need referruling before the engines had seen a month's service. His forecast proved correct. I was amused by his reference to 'tomato price', and as good tomatoes could be purchased in those days for 3*d.* per lb. or even less, I reckoned up what 74 tons 7 cwt. of tomatoes would cost; and once again Jock was correct!

Several of the engines were stationed at New Cross, and they regularly worked the best trains, such as the 5.5 pm to Eastbourne which made Lewes the first stop at 6.12. This train followed the 5 pm London Bridge to Brighton, which ran non-stop and was later known as the 'City Limited'. One evening No. 56 *Roberts* was booked for the 5.5, but shortly before time for leaving the shed she developed some fault which prevented her from doing the job. There was not another coupled engine in steam in the yard, but there were two single-wheelers, Nos. 331 *Fairlight* and 333 *Ventnor*, and 'the bloke' reckoned they would be able to manage the 5.5 between them, so they were hastily got ready and sent up to London Bridge. I've already mentioned that drivers of Stroudley engines were always eager to take a mickey out of any of old Bob Billinton's 'watercarts', and here was a chance too good to be missed.

There was a 'Gladstone' on the 5 o'clock as usual, and the driver of this was surprised when the two single-wheelers backed on to the 5.5 on the other side of the platform but he didn't half grin when the driver of the first one came over and asked him if he would mind keeping out of their way, as they were going to show old Bob how trains ought to be run. He said right, he would do his best, and duly departed on the dot. Meantime some of the regular passengers had got wind that something was happening, seeing two engines on their train. Well, to cut a long story short, promptly at 5.5, off went *Fairlight* and *Ventnor* on what proved to be the fastest run ever made by that particular train. Despite the fact that the 5 o'clock was running ahead of time, they were right on top of it at Hayward's Heath, as the down main distant was 'on' when the leading driver sighted it. They stopped at Lewes six minutes early, and would have been earlier than that, but for the service slack at Keymer Junction where the Eastbourne line diverges from the main Brighton line, after which there was no need for hurry, Lewes being only nine miles farther on. It was a pity that there were no stop-watch fanatics travelling on either train, they would have had the time of their lives!

A shining 'Grasshopper' No. 208 *Abercorn* in ex-Works condition raises steam in Brighton Works yard in 1904. It carries the post-1903 St Leonards shedcode at the side of the buffer beam.

Lens of Sutton

Chapter Fifteen

The Stop-Watch Specialist
is Taught a Lesson

Mention of stop-watch specialists reminded me of one - long since deceased - who wrote articles for the semi-technical press, extracts from which were frequently cut out by the Brighton enginemen, and stuck up on the wall of the lobby with appropriate comments! Rumour had it that he had been refused an apprenticeship by the leading railways, but was eventually accepted by a smaller one. Most folk have heard of the new office-boy who can run the business better than the managing director, and isn't afraid to say so; well, our hero was like that. He told everybody in the railway works how their jobs should be done, and nobody would work with him. Finally, after a complaint by the chief draughtsman, the locomotive superintendent called him into the office, and you can guess what he thought when the apprentice started lecturing him on locomotive design! It is hardly necessary to add that Mr Knowitall's premium was promptly returned, and the works knew him no more. After failing at several other jobs, he drifted into journalism.

His idea of a 'good' driver was one who could knock a few minutes off schedule, no matter if he ruin the big-ends, got all the axleboxes hot, and burnt the crown sheet of the firebox in doing so. To get material for his articles, he applied for engine passes, and on one of the occasions when he got one, he boarded the engine of a Victoria train at Brighton. It was during the holiday period, when everything that could turn its wheels was pressed into service. The engine was one of the Billinton 'Grasshoppers' (the small 4-4-0 type) which were nothing worth writing home about, even when in good fettle. I believe it was No. 208 *Abercorn*; anyway, she was due for heavy repairs, and would not have been on the road had it not been for urgent need.

Most of the LB&SCR drivers were dab hands at nursing a sick engine, and getting the best out of her without adding to her complaints, and the driver in this case was a real specialist. He had an excellent fireman, too, and that worthy had got a fairly good starting fire, so that the engine was blowing off at full pressure when they got the 'right-away', with Mr Knowitall in the cab. Despite the efforts of the fireman, and the careful handling of the driver, steam had fallen to 80 lb. by the time the engine was leaving Clayton Tunnel. The five-mile pull up the 1 in 264 grade from Brighton to the south end of the tunnel had run the poor old girl out of breath, but she had picked up a bit of speed on the down grade through the tunnel itself, which is a little over a mile long. Now with a shy steamer the only way to keep going, and to avoid a complete stop, is to take advantage of every scrap of down grade where the train will coast with steam off; so the driver shut the regulator and dropped into full gear (best position for coasting) while the fireman put the blower on, tickled up the fire, and got a drop more water into the boiler ready for the next bit of collar-work, up from Wivelsfield to the summit at the north end of Balcombe Tunnel.

When the driver shut off, Mr Knowitall immediately asked why, as the train was doing less than 50 mph and the driver replied, to blow up a bit for the climb to Balcombe. Speed dropped a little through Burgess Hill, where the grade eases out for a mile or so but when they passed Wivelsfield there was 140 lb. 'on the clock', and water up to the top of the gauge glass, so the driver opened out and notched up to about 50 per cent cut-off. The engine responded to the best of her ability but she was down to 80 lb. again, with the water near the bottom nut, as she struggled over the top of the grade at Balcombe Tunnel signal box. From this point the line falls mostly at 1 in 264 (20 ft per mile) to about ½ mile north of Horley, so the driver let her pick up speed to about 50 mph and then shut off again, for another blow up.

This didn't please Mr Knowitall at all, and he started telling the driver how to do his job. The driver naturally resented this, but he made no comment, and concentrated on his effort to keep going, while his mate repeated his attempt to get the steam pressure up again, and fill up the boiler for the next climb. The train was routed via the Quarry line, first stop East Croydon, and once they managed to get through Quarry Tunnel it was all plain sailing, as from that point it was downhill practically all the way to Victoria. By the time they hit the bottom of the bank just beyond Horley, steam was just below blowing-off pressure, and the driver opened out and let the engine go for it. She made a gallant effort, but the last bit at 1 in 200 up to the tunnel nearly finished her. However, she up managed it, and after letting her pick up speed a little, the driver shut off and coasted down to the stop at East Croydon, landing about 7 minutes late, not so bad under the circumstances.

During the stop, Mr Knowitall started lecturing the driver on his 'lack of enterprise' for not tearing down the grades under steam, and trying to rush the following up-grade, and so keeping time. If he had not lost his job at the railway works, he would have known all about the relationship of grade to drawbar drag, and that starting a climb at moderate speed with a full boiler and plenty of steam was a far surer way of getting to the top than attempting to rush it with low steam pressure and low water. The driver - I've forgotten his name - was a good-tempered sort of chap, and made no comment, but he determined to teach Mr Knowitall a lesson, and pay him in his own coin, in a manner of speaking. Steam pressure had not risen much on the coast down to East Croydon, as the fire was 'dirty' by now, with plenty of clinkers on the bars, but that didn't now matter, as there were no more long grades to climb.

When they got the 'right-away', the driver gave the sick engine all she had, to get the train on the move, and she slowly climbed the short hump past Windmill Bridge Junction to Selhurst. She accelerated down the steeper drop (1 in 100) to Thornton Heath, but this time the driver did not shut off, so she proceeded to make a frantic dash for home. Over the two little humps at Norbury and Streatham Junction North she went without checking, scooted around the wide curve to Balham, and went down the drop to Clapham Junction like a car on a switchback. As she raced through the station at a tidy lick, the driver could not resist a large size in grins, for in a matter of seconds, Mr Knowitall was going to be mighty sorry that he ever said anything about keeping steam on down the banks!

From Clapham Junction, going towards London, the line runs parallel with the old South Western for about a mile, still on a falling grade to Pouparts

Junction where the line divides. One part goes straight on to Stewarts Lane; the other diverges sharply to the right, then bears left on a rising gradient, crosses the bridge over the South Western lines, goes through Battersea Park station, crosses the river and drops down into Victoria. There is a 30 mph speed restriction through the junction, of which Mr Knowitall was well aware. As the junction rails are checked, and very carefully aligned, the junction can be taken at a much higher speed in perfect safety, but Mr Knowitall didn't know that. The driver did! He told me that as he made no attempt to reduce speed as the engine approached the junction, Mr Knowitall's face first went deathly white, then pale green, and his legs started shaking. He grabbed the cab pillar and clung on for dear life. The engine just gave one lurch as she took the junction, but that was all there was to it. She eased up on the rise to Battersea Park, where the driver shut off, braked down the drop into Victoria, and made a perfect two-application stop about three yards from the buffers. Mr Knowitall, trembling like a leaf, got off the engine and went staggering down the platform as if he had had 'one over the eight' - he never even said good-bye. The driver said he reckoned that experience ought to have cured him of trying to tell drivers how to do their job, especially with regard to keeping steam on down banks!

Incidentally, an article by another stop-watch merchant, whose conception of a 'good' driver coincided with that held by Mr Knowitall had a very unexpected sequel. This party boarded a London-bound train at Dover (SE&CR). The engine was a 'D' class 4-4-0, and soon after starting she developed a fault and had to come off the train at Faversham. The only available engine to take it on was an old 'C' class 0-6-0 goods engine which was doing a bit of shunting. Engines and crews were quickly exchanged, and the train proceeded, but the main line driver apparently overlooked the fact that an old goods engine was a different proposition to handle than a main line passenger engine, and proceeded to wallop the daylights out of her. He nearly blew the chimney off the smokebox going up Sole Street bank, and raced her down every grade, - touching just on 80 mph in the dip before Farningham Road, gaining a few minutes of the time lost.

The stop-watch merchant went into ecstasies over this 'good' driving, and in his next article heaped praise on the driver for his 'enterprise' giving his name. Unfortunately for that worthy, the chief mechanical engineer of the SE&CR happened to read the article, and promptly carpeted the driver for the damage he did to the old engine by running it at excessive speed. A British Railways class '9' with the same size driving wheels (5 ft) will run at over 80 mph, but there is a vast difference between a modern 2-10-0 properly balanced, with well-designed cylinders and motion, and an old 0-6-0 goods engine with hit-and-miss balancing, slide-valve cylinders and 'wet' steam. I wonder that she kept on the rails! Although the above incident did not take place on the LB&SCR it is worth recording, as it indicates the rummy ideas some folk have of what constitutes a 'good' driver.

Chapter Sixteen

Tommy, the Travelling Cat, and an Introduction to Valve Movements

In Michael Reynolds's book *Engine Driving Life* there is an account of a stray mongrel dog that found its way into Euston station one evening, and was 'adopted' by a driver. He called it Snatchbury, and it became so attached to him that it would ride on his engine, and knew its way about the LNWR. Well, Snatchbury had nothing on a cat that lived at New Cross depot in the years before the turn of the century. This cat, known as Tommy, had been sterilised in his kitten days, and had grown up into a beautiful creature, like a young tiger. His job was to keep the pits in the sheds free from rats, and if Tommy spotted one and got his teeth into it, that was the end of the rat's life story. He was 'on the staff', home being the stores, and was fed by the storekeeper; but he knew his way all over the Brighton system as well as any human being.

After his nightly patrol of the pits - he never neglected his duty! - he would pack up on the top of a tender for a quiet nap. As I mentioned the Stroudley engines had part of the exhaust steam turned into the tender to warm the feed water, and Tommy always selected a tender with a warm top, curling up close to the coping in the corner where it joined the coal partition. He was well known, of course, to all the drivers and firemen, and if they found him on the tender when about to leave the shed, they did not disturb him. When the engine went out, if Tommy had not finished his snooze, he just went with it, and that was that. If the weather was fine, he just finished his nap. If it was cold or rainy, he would come over the coal into the cab, and make himself comfortable on the seatbox between the side of the boiler backhead and the side of the cab. He never strayed, but would stay with the engine crew until they returned to the shed.

If the storekeeper put down Tommy's dinner, and later found it untouched, he would tell the office clerk that Tommy had hopped it again, and the clerk usually telephoned the other depots asking if they had seen our 'moggy' around their way. Maybe a reply would come from, say, Eastbourne, 'Yes, he's on Nobby Clark's engine, left here at 2.15'. As soon as the engine ran into the yard, Tommy was off it, making a bee-line for his dinner plate. The only time that he didn't come back hungry was when he had been to Newhaven, where the boys used to fill him up with fish.

At the period mentioned above, the sheds on Sunday afternoon were reminiscent of Goldsmith's 'Deserted Village'. No goods trains ran on Sundays, and very few passenger trains, consequently the sheds, and most of the yard, were full of 'dead' engines, silent and cold. The only signs of life were maybe three or four cleaners on the 1 pm to 8 pm shift, working on the first engines out on Monday morning, a couple of boiler-washers, and the driver and fireman of the yard pilot, who also acted as emergency reliefs in case somebody on the road suddenly got a pain in his tummy. Occasionally a fitter and mate would stay to finish a rush job, but that was all.

One Sunday afternoon I was on that shift with three other cleaners, and for company's sake, instead of doing our jobs separately we 'worked down'; that is all four of us worked together on each engine. By the time we had finished, there was still a couple of hours or so to go before knocking-off time and as there happened to be one engine with the fire alight, we made a can of 'brew' and sat up in the cab, to drink it and eat our 'tommy'. Conversation turned to the subject of how slide-valves opened and closed the steam and exhaust ports at different positions of the reverse gear. Two of the boys seemed rather hazy on the subject, and as there was an engine at the end of the shed with the steam-chest cover off, for having the portfaces trued up, I suggested that we did a bit of investigating. Incidentally, the job of truing up worn portfaces was one of the few piecework jobs, tedious and tricky. The old portfacer at New Cross - I believe his name was Ilsley - was a marvel of skill and patience. Several times I watched him cover his big surfaceplate with blue marking, apply it to the portface, then carefully scrape away at the cast iron, smoothing down the high spots indicated by the blue marking. It wanted some doing, in the cramped space between the cylinder bores. He told me that he got £3 per set, and he certainly earned it.

Well, we found a pinchbar and proceeded to investigate. For the enlightenment of the uninitiated, a pinchbar is a long heavy steel bar with a very short wedge-shaped end, bent over a little. By putting this end between the driving wheel and the rail, and pressing the other end down, one man can move an engine an inch or so at a time. One boy went up in the cab to operate the reversing wheel, two got busy on the pinchbar, and your humble servant watched the movement of the valves by aid of a torchlamp, yelling out 'Whoa!' as soon as the slide-valve cracked the front port. We then took note of the position of the cranks, and saw what happened when the reversing gear was operated. This was interesting indeed, so we proceeded to find out how far the piston travelled down the cylinder before the valve cut off steam, at various positions of the reverser; and it became quite clear how steam was saved by 'notching up'.

Anyway, to cut a long story short, we became so engrossed that we did not realise that we had a spectator (it was dusk outside, and the shed was badly lighted) until a voice wanted to know what the (blue-pencil) we were up to. It was 'the bloke's' understudy, the assistant district superintendent who had unexpectedly called in at the depot. We explained that having finished our cleaning, we were trying to make use of the time remaining before the end of the shift by learning something about valve movements. He grinned and said 'So that's it, is it? I can see we're going to have some damned good drivers on this road later on! Now tell me exactly what it is you want to know?' We did, and he promptly proceeded to hold an impromptu MIC (mutual improvement class), explaining why the valve had to be longer than the overall length of the ports, so that steam could work expansively when running, and why lead opening was necessary to enable steam to exert full pressure on the pistons at the instant the cranks passed the dead centres. We moved the engine under his direction, so that we could see the relative position of the valves and cranks. He also showed us how to test for leakage and blowing of valves and pistons. By setting the cranks and valve gear in certain positions, and opening the regulator slightly with brakes on, it was easy to locate whether a valve or piston was blowing, and which one. He stayed with us for about an hour, till the end of the shift and I can honestly say that it was the most interesting , instructive, and pleasant hour that I ever spent in the service of the LB&SCR. What I learned on that Sunday evening I have never forgotten, and the knowledge has been most useful, right down the years.

Now I'm afraid that the time has come to book off. I hope that my recollections of the railway that I loved so well have interested and amused you. Sometimes, when driving my little LB&SCR single-wheeler *Grosvenor* around my railway near Purley Oaks station, sighting the full-size signal from Coulsdon North giving me the all-clear as we take the curve, and hearing the rumble and clatter of a full-size train on top of the adjacent railway bank, the surroundings seem to fade out, the little engine suddenly 'grows up', and I am speeding once more through beautiful Sussex, on my way to the South Coast. It is so vivid that I have often wondered if it *is* only just a daydream, or an actual momentary return to the past. Strange things happen on this earth - who could say with certainty?

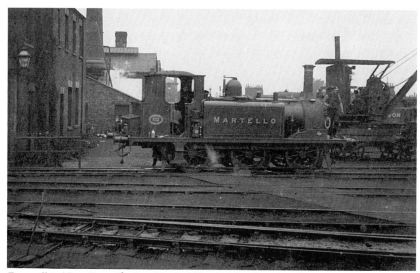

Farewell to New Cross Shed as 'Terrier' No. 62 *Martello*, taken from a less usual vantage point enabling a glance round the corner of the shed foreman's office. In view is the north frontage of the fitters' shop and behind it the smithy and the site of the later carriage and wagon repair shop. The ancient vertical boilered crane was used to assist at the coaling stage.   *M.P. Bennett/Bluebell Archives*

Appendix

Memories of the Bluebell Line

Whenever I am reminded of the Bluebell Line and of the treatment it received from the British Transport Commission, I always get a bad attack of nostalgia, mingled with indignation, for it was one of the first lines that I worked over in my footplate days on the London Brighton and South Coast Railway - which the kiddies called the Look-Bill-and-See-Charlie's-Rabbits. That was long before the days of road competition and although the traffic naturally did not match up to main or suburban line standards there was certainly plenty to keep us quite busy. One item was the milk traffic, and I recollect the 'milk stops' quite well.

One of the turns which included these was the 5.10 pm from Brighton. This train called at London Road 5.13, Falmer 5.21, Lewes 5.32, passed Culver Junction 5.40, called at Barcombe 5.45, Newick and Chailey 5.54, and Sheffield Park at 6.00 where six minutes were allowed for the milk churn stunt. Leaving at 6.06, we next called at Horsted Keynes at 6.16 for a two-minute breather, then went on to call at West Hoathly 6.23, Kingscote 6.29, landing at East Grinstead Low Level at 6.35, and we usually arrived on the dot!

As far as the public timetable was concerned, that was the end of the trip, but we still had plenty more to do. After milk churns, parcels and various other operations, which included firing up human boilers from the contents of tommy-bags and filling up from tea bottles, the train made a fresh start from East Grinstead at 7.02 pm. This was shown in the public timetable as a separate train, calling at Dormans 7.07, Lingfield 7.11 (two minutes stop), Oxted 7.24, Woldingham 7.31, Upper Warlingham 7.36, Sanderstead 7.44 (there was no Riddlesdown station in those days), Selsdon Road 7.47, South Croydon 7.49, East Croydon 7.52, Thornton Heath 7.58, Clapham Junction 8.10, Grosvenor Road 8.16 (two minutes stop for ticket collecting) and finishing at Victoria at 8.20 pm.

It can be seen from the above that the Bluebell Line, far from being just an insignificant branch, was actually part of an alternate through route between London and Brighton. Many of the Oxted line trains continued over it for the full distance. The fact that there was only a single line between Horsted Keynes and Culver Junction was no drawback. The intermediate staff stations were Sheffield Park and Newick and Chailey.

As a matter of fact, the bridges and other engineering features were all made to carry a double line, and it was understood among the Brighton engineers that the doubling would be only a matter of time, and that the line would then be used as an alternative to the main line. Even in those days the main line was very congested, despite the easing afforded by the then new Quarry line between Coulsdon and Earlswood. If the Bluebell Line were still LB&SCR this would have been done long ago and electric wires strung all along it. (The Brighton line used the overhead catenary system, very many years before British Railways dreamed about it). The old company was always well to the

Lawrence lived to see the day when two of his old favourites had their life expectancy extended when they steamed on into the era of railway preservation. On 27th October, 1963 *Stepney* and *Birch Grove*, one time contemporary stablemates at New Cross, charge past crowds of spectators at Ardingly double heading the 'Brighton Blue Belle' using the stock of the workmen's 'Lancing Belle'. The return journey back from Sheffield Park to Brighton was the last official passenger train over the Haywards Heath-Horsted Keynes branch before closure to traffic that same evening.

Bluebell Archives

'Brighton on Parade' on the Bluebell Line as *Birch Grove* and *Stepney* together shunt a service train onto the East Grinstead spur at Horsted Keynes which includes, nearest the camera, the recently arrived LB&SC Director's Inspection Saloon of 1914 during a 'Brighton Week' in September 1965.   *Tom Martin*

'All Creatures Great and Small!' *Stepney*, shunting up the Newick spur at Sheffield Park, and *Birch Grove* add to the Brighton image on a Sunday in July 1966.   *M.J. Mason*

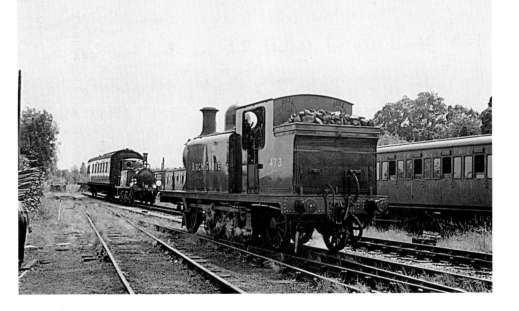

fore with improvements and innovation such as block signalling, electric lighting, electric passenger alarm bells, cheap excursions, season tickets and what-have-you.

There were also strong rumours that a new spur line would be laid in, starting just north of Culver Junction, running through Ringmer, to join the main line to Eastbourne and Hastings. This would have provided a shorter route between London and those towns, than the one via Haywards Heath and Lewes. It makes me feel very sad indeed to think of the old line now lying silent and deserted, when things might well have been so different.

There are two ways of dealing with a line that doesn't pay. The one favoured by British Railways is to abandon it, but the LB&SCR way was to provide cheap and frequent services to attract both goods and passenger traffic. The services on the Bluebell Line provided by BR were little short of ridiculous since very few trains at inconvenient times simply force passengers to take to the roads. My own solution would have been to get two or three railbuses on the job between Lewes and East Grinstead, each with a driver and conductor, operating just like a road bus, taking fares on board. These would have run at frequent intervals from early morning to late evening, and would have carried parcels in addition to passengers. As well as using the existing stations, request stops could have been arranged at every point where the line intersected a public road, near farms, groups of cottages - in fact at any point which might be convenient to prospective passengers. Some contrast to the miserable four-trains-a-day business, run at times when nobody wanted to travel.

In addition to the railbuses, there would have been through trains between London and Brighton, morning, evening and week-ends, calling at the Bluebell Line stations, and a morning and evening milk special. Freight traffic could have been dealt with either by diverting some of the existing goods trains between London and South Coast towns, or running a local service to connect with them. I'm pretty sure that with a little intelligent organisation, the Bluebell Line could not only have held its own against road competition, but flourished like the bluebells and primroses growing along its route.